De-Mystify Investing

Master the Teeter Totter Principle

Profit in Both Up & Down Markets

Terry J. Atzen

Absolute Author

Publishing House

Publisher: Absolute Author Publishing House
Editor: Dr. Melissa Caudle
Associate Editor: Kathy Rabb Kittok
Cover Designer: Rebeca @Rebecacovers

LIBRARY OF CONGRESS CATALOGUE IN-PUBLICATION-DATA

De-Mystify Investing/Terry J. Atzen

p. cm.

Paperback ISBN: 978-1-64953-123-0

eBook ISBN: 978-1-64953-124-7

1. Finance   2. Investing   3. Stock Market   4. Financial Investing

Testimonials

"De-Mystify Investing: Master the Teeter Totter Principle and Profit in both Up and Down Markets is an exclusive and one-of-a-kind guide to buying, selling and achieving success in the stock market." **Karem B., Whitefish, MT**

Terry has come up with an extraordinary roadmap that anyone can follow while discovering the magic of Point-and-Figure charts and how to interpret them. My need for a stockbroker has basically vanished. **Gerry P., Cambria, CA**

I wish I had this incredible tool 25 years ago! **Margaret W., Kalispell, MT**

TABLE OF CONTENTS

Introduction

Nearly 100 years ago, Will Rogers first "De-Mystified," investing when he said, "The way to make money in the stock market is to buy a stock. Then, when it goes up, sell it. If it does not go up, don't buy it."

Remember, Mr. Rogers was a comedian; I am not.

As years passed for me and the more I read that quote, the more I considered that at least he was on the right track and that the part about what to do if your stock went up made sense to me.

But after reading the second part, I, like most folks, laughed and probably said something like, "I wish it were that simple."

Sure, everything was different when Mr. Rogers made this comment, and I guess that things will continue to change. Markets change as world events change, and markets change as regulatory changes are made; there is always a "reason" for change.

The most significant change for me was not the economic changes but the technological tools that have been created. I recognized this massive amount of technological advancement might be the key to help produce investment success for investors.

The early focus that was going on always seemed to be on the economic changes, not so much on developing technical, analytical tools. That focus has lasted for decades.

It wasn't until I pealed through the many layers of "noise" that's out there that clarity finally came.

Trust me, there is a lot of noise from the media, market pundits, market "expert," and proponents of the "It's-a-Difficult-Marketplace" myth.

After that, I developed my simple, logical tool and produced excellent results.

Change always created lots of questions and brought on only more confusion and doubt. From the beginning, investing has always intrigued me.

So, when I looked up the meaning of the word intrigue to see if it fit my investment description, it came as no surprise that there wasn't just one meaning, but two meanings. Look.

Intriguing

- ✓ Interesting
- ✓ Fascinating
- ✓ Absorbing
- ✓ Compelling
- ✓ Gripping
- ✓ Riveting
- ✓ Captivating
- ✓ Engaging
- ✓ Enthralling
- ✓ Diverting
- ✓ Titillating
- ✓ Tantalizing
- ✓ Stimulating
- ✓ Thought-Provoking

Boy, those sure fit how I felt! Then, I found that intriguing could also mean:

- ✓ Plot
- ✓ Hatch A Plot
- ✓ Conspire
- ✓ Take Part in A Conspiracy
- ✓ Make Secret Plans

- ✓ Lay Plans
- ✓ Scheme
- ✓ Maneuver
- ✓ Connive
- ✓ Collude
- ✓ Work Hand in Glove
- ✓ Complot
- ✓ Cabal
- ✓ Machinate

Isn't it interesting that the second definition turns the first meaning from what I call "a fastball" into a "curveball" so that all I had to learn was first to recognize what a curveball looked like, and second, learn how to hit it?

Combining the above two definitions, I have come up with my own - Investing, a captivatingly, riveting maneuver of money. That's it! That's what investing is!

And, if that is the case, no wonder there are so many investors in the world who don't know how to, why to, when to, where to, and what to, when it comes to investing or investment strategies.

Then, to make matters more complicated, many investors add their "inner voice" to the dialogue, that the investment process is too complicated for them and that they aren't smart enough. They think they have to "know the 'right' broker," have an "insider" in their back pocket, or they "leave the decisions to a professional."

It amazes me that more isn't written to provide investors alternative solutions regarding these types of questions.

There were no factual questions or answers when I began my career as an investor. I started investing because I had nothing better to do with the raise I got when I was promoted from an Ensign to a Lt. Junior Grade in the Navy, **sixty** years ago, and I was at sea most of the time.

For decades after that, I continued to invest in the same way. It was usually because someone else told me, "It was the thing to do." Whether it was an individual stock, a mutual fund, or a private investment, "it was the thing to do."

So, that is what I did!

Sure, I have made some significant investments, and they made fabulous profits for me, and by the same token, I also made plenty that didn't. I never attempted to analyze the difference, so investing remained a mystery to me, and it didn't bother me until years later.

Then one day, I asked myself, "What the heck is going on? Why am I not consistently making profits? Why am I always worried about nearly every investment I make?" Why did I always doubt the investment decisions I made? What was I afraid of? Why was there self-doubt?

My educational background is science, and that is why my approach to investing is scientific and does not follow the concepts of what is normally accepted by the financial world.

Henry Thoreau said it best, "Simplify, simplify." And then my favorite quote from Albert Einstein, "If you can't explain it to a 6-year-old, you don't understand it yourself."

What if investing was simple? What if investing wasn't as complicated as many portrayed it to be? How can the investment process be made so that anyone could understand it?

These are the questions I began to explore, and when I employed this line of questioning, the entire concept of making investment decisions changed dramatically for me.

Uncovering an investment process that was sound, logical, and simple became my goal and passion - that is what this book will show you.

What follows did not come to me all at once, rather, my work has evolved. Through trial and error (a scientific phenomenon) my work has taken me to where I am now. Nevertheless, the questions keep coming – and I continue to ask more and more questions.

Tony Robbins has said, "Successful people ask better questions, and as a result, they get better answers."

What if there was a logical, easy-to-understand and simple method to use when making an investment decision?

My answer is, "There is!"

This book reveals what I have discovered, what I use as my methodology, and the rationale supporting my work.

Let's get started!

Welcome to my world!

Terry J. Atzen

Chapter 1

Investing vs Gambling

There is still much discussion about what investing is. Many believe that investing is nothing more than gambling.

Nothing could be further from the truth.

Both gambling and investing involve risks, but the similarity ends there.

With gambling, there are what is call "the odds." What that means is that if you place the bet, you have ten chances that you'll lose in contrast to only one chance that you'll win.

With gambling, you lose to "the house," and, in our example, you will lose ten times. The one time that you win, you win because you are lucky, nothing else.

Some people believe that they can beat the odds; however, they can't; it's impossible.

The odds are always against the gambler and in favor of the house, but people like to gamble because they want to hope that their return will be as large as their loss is if they hit it lucky.

When investing, as opposed to a bet, one is also putting the money at risk; however, that risk, investment risk can be mitigated or reduced. With gambling, risk cannot be mitigated.

Mitigating risk is accomplished with investing and is best summed up by one word, diversification.

It virtually guarantees investors diversification when investing in Index Funds, Global Funds, and Sector Funds while keeping balanced among the various funds.

The investment methodology I recommend uses these funds and others. It is an easy guide to follow for all investors.

The thing to always keep in mind is that what I teach is not a trading program. We focus on investing in long-term results. The markets are used to make large moves, up and down, over long periods, often lasting for many weeks or months.

The basic intent is to determine the direction a market is taking, up or down, and staying with that trend until it changes direction.

Recognizing those changes, up from down and vice versa, will become your biggest challenge. Once the course of action is determined, it's as simple as staying on that course until the next change.

That is what long-term investing is all about.

Investing is a process with known input and with a planned outcome.

Gambling is just a single event.

This book is about a proven process.

Chapter 2

A Question for You

"It is not the answer that enlightens, but the question." **Eugene Ionesco**

Here's a question for you. What if you found out that investing can be worry-free and that it isn't as difficult or tricky as you have always thought?

And what if I told you that not being smart enough, not being wealthy enough, not being worthy of or deserving of the benefits of taking control of your wealth-building are all myths?

Many investors believe these myths to be true, but that is all they are, just myths! Yes, nothing more than widely held but false ideas.

What if you found out, after all this time, which thinking investing was too complicated (or fill-in-the-blank), and that successful investing boils down to learning just "one thing?"

Yes, I said, just "One thing."

If you learn and apply the implications of just this "one thing," you can become a successful investor.

Later in this book, I will reveal that "one thing" and give you a clear road map to follow. However, before going there, I'd like to discuss another point.

As an investment coach, my job is to find investors who want to expand their understanding of markets and hopefully improve their investment results, regardless of their investing experience.

I want to engage with people that will open their minds to new concepts and expand their sphere of experiences

Let's begin by exploring this question. What is investing, and why do we invest?

We invest to accumulate funds earmarked for some specific future event, funds for a new car, funds for a down payment on a new home, or education.

However, the most common reason people invest is to create their retirement nest egg. As you know, no one else is going to do that for you. Many people have found out the hard way that the government's retirement fund, called Social

Security, is not an adequate retirement plan and falls short of what the average American requires.

Creating our retirement funds is the responsibility of each of us. And the sooner we start with that plan, the better. Time is your best friend as you accomplish this goal.

But the real reason we need to invest in that is that if we don't, there is this big boogeyman out there called inflation. As you probably know, inflation is historically low.

But you need to understand that it's like we are having interest rates and inflation are equal. There is no way that we can build a retirement nest egg when that is the case. Savings only keep us even with the game.

Okay, I know that besides that boogeyman, there is also an enormous elephant in the room for investing; there is RISK!

And isn't it true that investing is risky?

Absolutely!

Risk exists everywhere. There are natural disaster risks. There are accidents and illnesses, international unrest, political changes, and, yes, plain ol' human errors that loom as investment risks. Investors must face these and more.

Knowing this, risks can be mitigated, which is what this book is all about: mitigating risk.

So, the only chance we have to eliminate the risk of investing is to search for the "Ideal Investment."

I know that folks believe that is impossible, and they may be right, however, let's see how close we can get to describing what an ideal investment looks like.

I believe that the ideal investment should have the following ingredients:

1. **Liquidity** - meaning it can be turned into cash quickly.
2. **Diversification** - meaning there is a wide range of products.
3. **Little or No Correlation** - meaning a reduced connection between investment vehicles.
4. **Be Simple** - meaning understandable, like "One Thing."
5. **Tell Me When to Buy and Not to Buy** - knowing when to hold 'em and when to fold 'em
6. **Be Easy to Manage** - meaning fewer decisions.
7. **Have Low Fees** - which means savings.
8. **Income** - meaning some cash in your pocket.
9. **Good Performance** - beating the "averages."

My goal is to include these ingredients as I proceed through my methodology.

Chapter 3
Getting Started

"A journey of a thousand miles begins with a single step." **Lao-Tzu, philosopher**

Investing is like any other journey. It begins with a single step.

The investment steps that investors have taken for the last ten years have been relatively easy.

Most investors have done well; however, because of that fact, investors (both amateurs and professionals) have unfortunately become complacent and apathetic since the beginning of our current pandemic.

As a result, I am afraid that many have "let their guard" down and assume that from that point on, everything will be the same when it is announced that the pandemic is "over."

As an investor, I categorically disagree.

Investors are well-advised to chart an alternative path.

This book has laid out a roadmap for investors to follow as a sound and rational re-beginning for all investors.

In my short eBook, *Post-Pandemic Investing: What Now?* I shared my belief that "The Law of Supply and Demand" should be the first step of every investor's decision-making process.

I have developed an investing methodology built around supply and demand that is powerful, yet simple, our economic system's principle.

The Law of Supply and Demand is the basic building block of everything we produce, from gadgets to groceries, including investment strategies.

My favorite technical analyst and author of *Point and Figure Charting*, Thomas Dorsey, wrote, "In its most simplistic form, the 'Irrefutable Law of Supply and Demand' reigns supreme. If there are more buyers than sellers willing to sell, the price must rise. If there are more sellers than buyers willing to buy, the price must decline to embrace the simplicity of this because it is all there is."

These are powerful and meaningful words, "...it is all there is."

The Law of Supply and Demand is the bedrock of my work. It is the only principle I apply to all of my investments. If there are more buyers than sellers, the investment we are considering will go up. If there are more sellers than buyers, the price will go down.

Nothing else matters. Nothing else needs to be considered. And I mean nothing!

My methodology's good news is that there is a perfect pictorial (a picture is worth a thousand words) representing supply and demand related to investing.

That representation is called a Point and Figure (PNF) chart. That is the ONLY purpose of the PNF chart, showing whether buyers are predominate or sellers. I will show you how to become a successful investor by using PNF charts to guide you.

The PNF is a roadmap for an investor to follow to determine who is dominating a market, buyers, or sellers.

I have authored this book to show how this same law can apply to every **investment decision** you will make using PNF charts.

The strategy works with the following markets I recommend you take part in:

1. US Stocks
2. US Bonds
3. Gold/Silver
4. Crude Oil
5. Real Estate
6. Foreign Stocks
7. US Dollar
8. Global Commodities

Taking part in these eight markets gives you one ingredient of the ideal investment discussed earlier, diversification.

Before we move on, let me show you where you can view every PNF chart that has ever been created. To see these, visit the website: www.stockcharts.com.

They are free!

Once on the site, click the drop-down menu of all of the charts this company created. They also frequently add new charts. In the drop-down, one of the choices will be "Point and Figure" – choose it. That will open a window that allows you to choose a specific chart you'd like to view. For example, if you want to look at the PNF chart of the S&P 500, type in their symbol – in this case, SPY.

Here is a table of the eight markets that I will be using and the symbol to put in the window:

Market Component	Index	ETF	Inverse ETF
US Stocks	S&P 500	SPY	SH
US Bonds	30-Year Govt Bonds	TLT	TBT
Energy	Crude Oil	UCO	SCO
Gold	Spot Gold	GLD	GLL
Foreign Stocks	EAFA Index	EFA	EFU
Commodities	S&P, GSCI Commodity Index	GSG	CMD
US Dollar	US Dollar	UUP	UDN
US Real Estate	DJ US Real Estate Index	VNQ	SRS

For many years, I have studied both fundamental and technical analysis. Both have their value.

Fundamental analysis is about using data to evaluate an investment. Using data, such as a corporation's revenues, earnings, future growth, return on equity, profit margins, the management team, and a company's competitive advantage with stock analysis, are examples of areas studied with fundamental analysis.

Technical analysis looks at statistics such as prices, price changes, and volume of trading plots, this data on chart paper, and looks for patterns that might develop.

After many years, I have focused primarily on technical analysis. Technical analysis focuses on "what is" and "what has been," whereas fundamental analysis focuses on "what will be."

With that being said, even as a technical analyst, I have an open mind and an eye on certain fundamental facts.

To illustrate, I refer to another favorite technical analyst of mine, Chris Vermeulen of *The Technical Trader*. Despite his being a technical trader, I can tell by what he recently wrote that he too monitors fundamental issues specifically, on what he describes as the current solvency issue:

> "The Solvency question equates to this simple issue... How can individuals, companies, states, and other entities continue to operate with greatly reduced income/revenues, moderately high debts, and liabilities throughout a process of an extended shutdown? Certainly, the option of adding more debt to ease the short-term

pain of lost revenues may be a solution, but we believe this issue is much bigger than these traditional short-term solutions. We believe the COVID-19 virus event is presenting a shift in traditional thinking for many economists, individuals, and enterprises."

This was written in mid-May 2020 and is one of the fundamental issues that haunt me daily and is one issue that, unfortunately, cannot be put on any technician's chart.

Chapter 4
The One Thing

"If you have an apple and I have an apple, and we exchange these apples, then you and I will still each have one apple. But if you have an idea and I have an idea, and we exchange these ideas, then each of us will have two ideas." **George Bernard Shaw**

———— ❦ ————

Now, for the next step. What you have all been waiting for, right? The one thing!

Trust me on this and let this part of my "message" really sink in!

Here it is!

If there are more buyers than sellers, that item's price will go up; conversely, if there are more sellers than buyers, that item's cost will go down. It's called the Law of Supply and Demand!

Nothing else matters at this point. The Law of Supply and Demand is irrefutable; it is always in effect, still!

It's in effect at the auto dealerships, it's in effect at the grocery store, it's in effect when you buy anything, and it's in effect when you buy stocks and bonds.

Think about it!

If you ever get a tattoo, this is one I recommend for investors. If a tattoo is not your style, at least print these words somewhere so that when you invest, remind yourself of this first, The Law of Supply and Demand!

When I started my career at Merrill Lynch, we had what we called the "Broker-of-the Day." This person's duty for that day was to take call-ins and answer questions from would-be investors. When I could not find a reason in *The Wall Street Journal* for "Why is IBM up today?" I would make one up. However, as I was hanging up the phone, I would murmur (so as not to be heard), "There are more buyers than sellers," that's the real reason IBM was up that day.

This 'one thing' concept has remained in the back of my mind ever since. At first, I said it as a joke, but the more I thought about it, the more I became convinced that it is the only valid statement and that it has far more meaning than first meets the eye.

Okay, let's go more in depth with stocks, mutual funds, bonds, and ETFs. Ask again, "Why do they go up in price or down in price?"

Most people will answer that its earnings, or a new product, or interest rates changing, or _____ (fill in the blank).

And we can come up with many answers. However, only one is irrefutable; it's whether there's a predominance of buyers or a predominance of sellers on that day.

It's as simple as that, The Law of Supply and Demand the 'one thing.'

What buyers and sellers do determine the price of everything, including stocks, bonds, commodities, real estate, yes, even Cadillacs.

Whenever I reveal this 'one thing' in front of an audience, I always pause for a moment, like when a comedian pauses for laughter. And sometimes, I get a laugh when I tell audiences there is only 'one thing' that determines the price of a stock. But at other times, I see the astonishment in the audience's eyes as they think about how simple that answer is. I always suppose that some are thinking, "It can't be THAT simple." While others are thinking, "OMG, that's true; it is that simple!"

If you're one of those that laugh at my premise, I urge you not to stop reading. This book is a quick read, and I only ask that you read further. If you're saying, "Oh, I know all about point-and-figure charts, they aren't all that important," please read on because there is a lot more that I need to tell you, and a lot more you need to consider. The PNF chart tells us way more than the majority gives them credit for.

What's most important about the 'one thing' is that only one can predominate at a time. There can only be a predominance of buyers or a predominance of sellers. If there is not a predominance of one or the other, that stalemate is called a "consolidation" and no direction of a trend is confirmed.

An uptrend is the predominance of buyers, and a downtrend is the predominance of sellers.

So, who are these buyers and sellers?

Well, they are all of us. They are the big traders, the institutions, even governments (QED) that move large blocks of stocks, bonds, commodities, etc. They are the banks, the mutual funds, hedge fund managers, algorithmic traders, individual investors, and governments taking part in daily stock and bond purchases.

From my perspective, it's not essential to know who the buyers or sellers are, and also every bit as unimportant to understand why they're buying or selling. A former mentor of mine taught me the answer to the "Why" question deserves the cosmic booby price; it simply doesn't matter why it is merely!

I find most remarkable about these transactions between buyers and sellers is that they are continually taking place, every minute, every second of every trading day. I look at that moment as a 'magic moment,' a moment they arrive at an exactly **opposite** investment decision, at precisely the same moment in time.

One is buying the investment, and one is selling the same investment at precisely the same moment. Who is correct? Who is incorrect?

I maintain that it does not matter who is correct or incorrect.

Some may think this is an oversimplification of this whole issue. Perhaps it is. Nevertheless, I remain steadfastly committed to the concept of "one thing."

The fact is that they are doing what they are doing, buying, or selling in keeping with their own goals, objectives, computer programs, or in line with their prospectus or charter.

Many of these large investors have their research departments or purchase research from an independent source. Many individual investors can purchase research.

From the beginning, though, I want readers to understand that I have tremendous respect for all the fundamental research that is done around the world. I am continuously amazed at the sheer volume of research that is available to us.

Investors, first, must make a series of decisions. The first decision is whether to invest at all. After that, the question is in which markets to invest. Then there is the timing issue.

With real estate, it is said that one of the most important factors is location, location, location, with investing, it's timing, timing, timing.

Professional investors, such as mutual funds, foundations, money managers, and hedge funds, mostly have well- defined investment parameters, either by prospectus or charter, not so much timing.

Individual investors can also benefit from having a fundamental investment strategy. However, an investment strategy differs from investment parameters that must be met when written down in a prospectus.

Here is another big difference: individual investors do

not necessarily have to take the risk of making personal stock selections if they invest in the stock market.

Likewise, individual investors do not risk selecting individual bonds if they wish to invest in the bond market. Individual investors can purchase a diversified portfolio of stocks or bonds by purchasing what is called an Exchange Traded Fund – an ETF.

Later in this book, we discuss the Exchange-Traded Funds (ETFs) in more detail and how they eliminate the need for us to take the risk of buying individual stocks and bonds. That feature also applies to other asset classes such as real estate, foreign stocks, and commodities.

Think about it, buy one ETF, such as SPY, and you will own 500 companies! Not just any 500 stocks, you'll own the 500 that represent the Standard & Poor's 500 Index! How great is that?

Or, how about owning all US Treasury ETF, TLT? This ETF contains a broad-spectrum of US Treasury bonds with various coupons and maturity dates, which reduces risk even further because of diversification.

By choosing to invest in ETFs, one eliminates one of the biggest challenges for investors, deciding which stock/bond to buy, which stock sector? Which maturity of bond?

All questions of this nature are answered by one investment decision, invest using ETFs.

Simple.

And, since I brought up the subject of ETFs, there is what we call Inverse ETFs – they go, as the name implies, in just the opposite direction of the ETF.   The real power of the Inverse ETF is that they enable us to profit when a market is going down.

If one has a system that can profit when stocks, bonds, etc. are going up and profit when they go down, then the entire investment process changes significantly, and I mean, significant!

If a market is going up, buy the 'long' ETF. If the market is going down, buy the inverse ETF.

Simple, logical, and essential!

Armed with all the above pieces, they can be put together to make investment decisions.

If you are ready to apply a refreshingly unique observation of the irrefutable Law of Supply and Demand to your investment decisions, then keep reading.

Again, these strategies were developed using the perfect, pictorial representation of The Law of Supply and Demand; The Point-and-Figure (PNF) chart.

This book is not intended to teach you how the PNF chart is made. It will clearly show you how to use this valuable tool.

There are three steps that I take with every investment I make and always in this sequence.

Step #1

Look at the PNF chart Index, first.

Learn about and checkout the PNF chart of the Index of the market you are analyzing.

This first step is taking "a view from 30,000 feet."

This step gives one a good view that many investors overlook. This is an important step, and it surprises me to see that it isn't discussed more in other investing disciplines.

Since you cannot invest in the Index itself, one must look to its surrogate, the ETF.

Step #2

Next, look at the PNF chart of the ETF that represents the sector you are considering. You are looking for confirmation of the signal that the chart of the Index is giving you.

If the PNF chart of the ETF agrees with the chart of the Index, then move on to the chart of the applicable Inverse ETF.

If the ETF chart of the ETF does not agree with the Index's chart, there is no trade.

Simple!

Step #3

However, when there is an agreement with the ETF and the Inverse ETF when the ETF is going up, and the Inverse is going down, then the Teeter Totter Principle comes into play.

The same is true if the ETF is going down, and the Inverse ETF goes up; there is still agreement as to the direction of the market one is considering.

What is critical is that all three of these charts must agree as to the direction of the market.

Teeter totters are irrefutable! When one end goes up, the other must go down and vice versa – you know how teeter totters work!

You are probably wondering why you have never heard of the Teeter Totter Principle.

Well, you haven't heard of it because, to the best of my knowledge, I created the term and no one has ever used the phrase before me.

So, here it is - when the three PNF charts of an investment agree as to the direction (up or down) of that investment, the ETF goes up, and the Inverse ETF goes down.   And, when the ETF goes down, the Inverse ETF goes up.

When one end of the teeter totter goes up, the other MUST go down (and vice versa).

If that is not the case, and both the ETF and the Inverse ETF are going in the same direction, something is out of balance, and there is no "Teeter" and no "Totter" so, therefore, no signal (either the buy or sell) is generated.

And so, it is with buyers and sellers of any investment.

It can't be any other way; it's as simple as that! That's all you need to know.

Let me show you a pictorial example to help clarify. Please note, that the **variances in lighter gray**, are the indicators. This holds true for the remainder of each chart and graph throughout the book.

I will show you an example using the Gold market when the direction of gold's price is confirmed by the PNF charts of all three charts - the Index, the ETF, and the Inverse ETF.

$GOLD Gold - Continuous Contract (EOD) CME
25-Aug-2020, 14:30 ET, daily, O: 1,935.90, H: 1,944.10, L: 1,919.10, C: 1,923.10, V: 25112000, Chg: -16.10 (-0.83%)
No recent chart pattern found

Scaling: Traditional [Reversal: 3]

(c) StockCharts.com

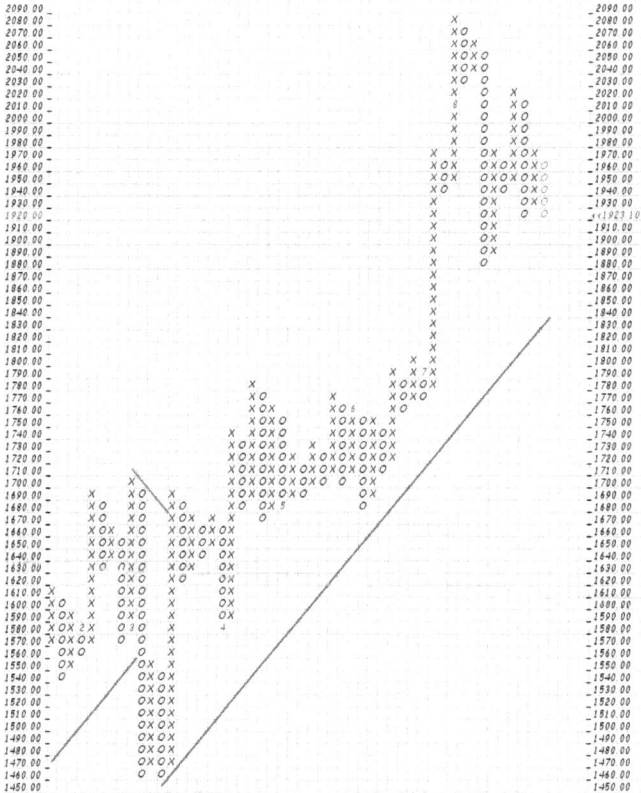

As you can see, the chart of the Index is in an uptrend.

Next, we look at the PNF chart of the ETF:

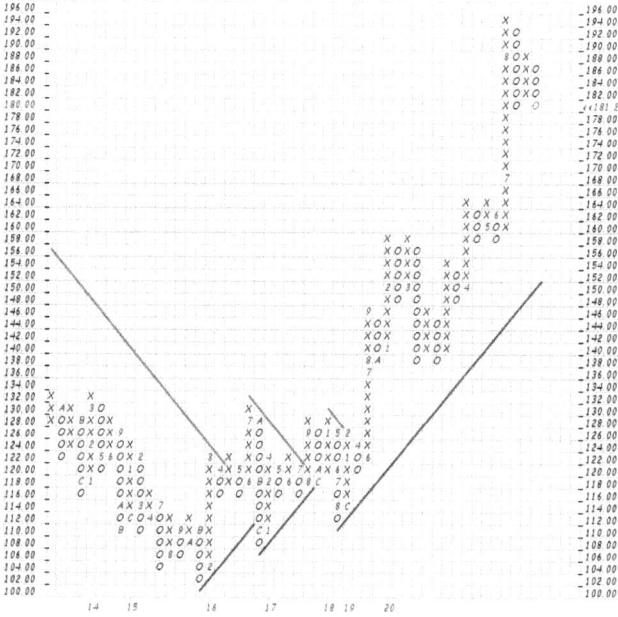

GLD SPDR Gold Shares NYSE
25-Aug-2020, 16:00 ET, daily, O: 181.06, H: 181.25, L: 179.731, C: 181.22, V: 10027657, Chg: +0.22 (0.12%)
No recent chart pattern found

Scaling: Traditional [Reversal: 3]

The ETF is also continuing its uptrend and giving us the agreement with the chart of the Index that we need.

And finally, the PNF chart of the Inverse ETF:

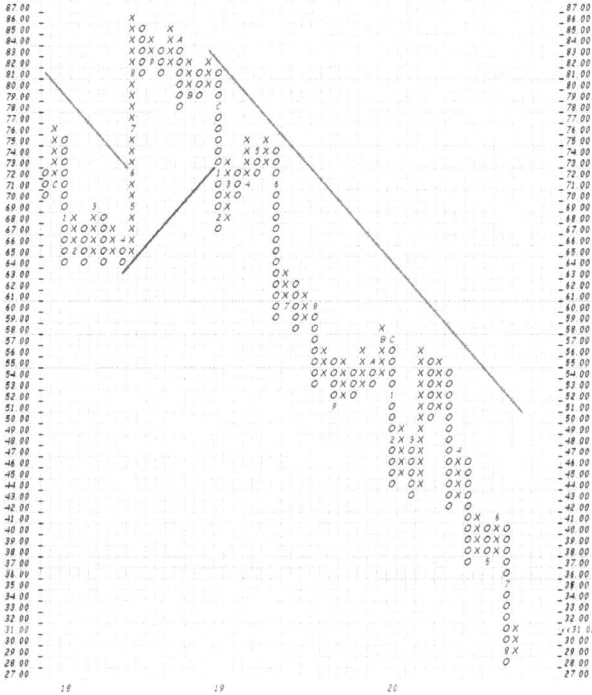

GLL ProShares UltraShort Gold NYSE
25-Aug-2020, 16:00 ET, daily, O: 31.10, H: 31.52, L: 31.02, C: 31.02, V: 185450, Chg. -0.05 (-0.16%)
No recent chart pattern found

Scaling: Traditional [Reversal: 3]

The Inverse ETF chart gives us the third and final chart that we are looking at, confirming the direction of the price of gold.

When you see the "agreement," you have all the information you need for an investment decision. Then you move on to the next sector of your portfolio and repeat the same process.

So, what is the simplest way to invest? My choice of investment vehicles is called an Exchange Traded Fund (ETF), as I mentioned earlier.

You need to be warned that some ETFs are "leveraged," meaning it is an ETF that uses debt or financial derivatives to boost their returns. The more the leverage an ETF has, the more volatility the ETF will have.

Please check with each ETF to be sure you know which are leveraged and which ones are not.

But ETFs offer much more diversification over selecting just one issue in any sector.

As I pointed out earlier, by purchasing the ETF, SPY, I own all 500 stocks in that Index. In bonds, by purchasing the ETF, TLT, I own an entire US Bond portfolio, not just one bond, or one stock.

This strategy/methodology works with the following markets:

1. Stock Market
2. Bond Market
3. Crude Oil
4. Gold and Silver
5. Foreign Equities
6. Real Estate

7. US Dollar
8. Global Commodities

These eight markets are used because they **all** have four attributes in common:

- ✓ They are all vast markets and include a large
  portion of our economy and offer much diversification.

- ✓ They each have in Index, and there is a PNF chart of that Index.

- ✓ They each have an ETF that corresponds to the Index and a PNF chart of that ETF, and

- ✓ They each have an Inverse ETF and a PNF chart that represents that corresponding Inverse ETF.

Chapter 5
POINT-AND-FIGURE CHARTS

"I don't care half so much about making money as I do about making my point and coming out ahead." **Cornelius Vanderbilt**

This chapter is not intended to teach you everything you need to know about PNF charts. I plan to give you enough to get started.

There are very few "rules" to follow, and I will discuss only the basics here.

In my career, I have looked at millions of PNF charts. I am convinced that repetition really is the mother of all learning and remains the best tool for mastering this fantastic tool.

PNF charts are not complicated. I urge you to continue your practice.

The Point-and-Figure (PNF) charts are the classic graphic representation of supply and demand. This is important because it is, after all, supply and demand that determines whether something goes up or down in price.

So, first, since we have decided that buyers and sellers (Law of Supply and Demand) are the cause that prices go up and down, the next step is to look at this information (what the buyers and sellers are doing); basically, the only data on a PNF chart.

That information is all they show, and that's why I use them exclusively. Many of you may not even know what a PNF is.

As a side-point of interest, the PNF charts were first written about in the 1880s. Yes, over 130 years ago.

And it may also interest you; they were first used (as the story goes) by a young journalist by the name of Charles Dow. Yes, that Charles Dow, the co-founder of Dow Jones & Company and founder of *The Wall Street Journal, Barrons,* and the Dow Theory, to mention just a few of his accomplishments.

Mr. Dow tracked stocks that he was interested in by writing numbers in the palm of his hand (that way, he didn't have to carry paper around) that represented the stock's price, whereas today Xs and Os are used.

Talk about coming full circle!

Today we can do the same thing, have P&F charts in

the palm of our hand. However, today, they're there electronically, minute by minute, via our smartphones!

How Cool Is That!

This is where 'the Art of Investing' begins and where the 'Art of Investing' should be discussed. I haven't mentioned this before now, but I'll tell you that interpreting what one sees in a PNF chart will become an art. It's not a science. Each of us may see a PNF chart differently.

Despite attempting to keep things simple, there are, unfortunately, a few "accepted" rules like:

Double Tops/Double Bottoms

Triple Tops/Triple Bottoms

Catapult formations/Triangle formations

Spread Triple Tops/Shakeout formations

Signal/Reversed Patterns

Please don't get bogged down with these terminologies. It's not the purpose of this book to teach you how PNF charts are created or teach you the finer points of reading the charts. Dorsey Wright (www. dorseywright.com) offers an excellent course on PNFCharting and is available online at no charge. I highly recommend that you take the course.

I do, however, want you to have the 'big picture' that PNF charts offer.

To begin with, when looking at a PNF chart, perhaps for the first time, you'll see a series of columns of Xs and Os. The Xs represent an upmarket or buyers in control of a market, while the column of Os shows that sellers are in control of a market. This is what's important for now.

As an example, below is a current PNF chart of the S&P 500 ETF, SPY.

SPY SPDR S&P 500 ETF NYSE
20-Sep-2017, 14:43 ET, daily, O: 250.07, H: 250.19, L: 248.92, C: 249.13, V: 28486608, Chg: -0.84 (-0.34%)
P&F Pattern Ascending Triple Top Breakout on 11-Jul-2015
Scaling: Traditional [Reversal: 3]

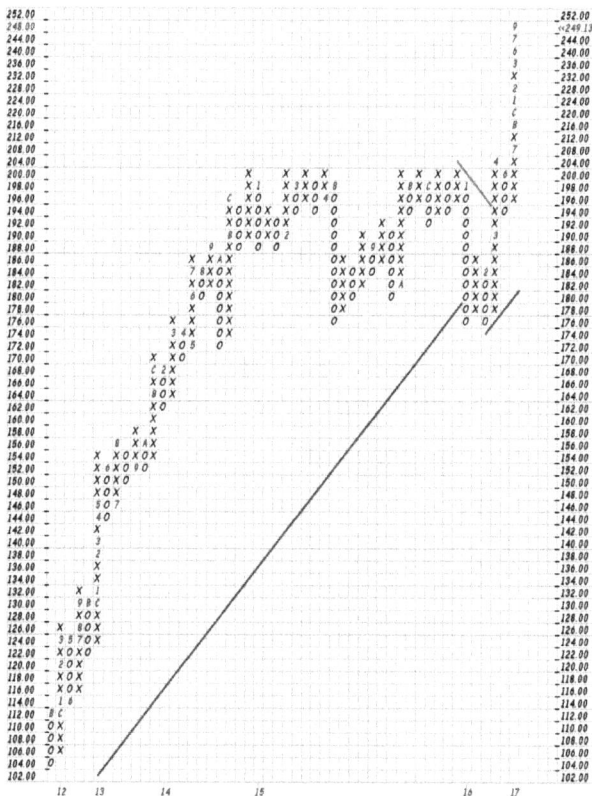

(c) StockCharts.com

As seen, since 2012 (the years are along the bottom of the chart), the chart shows many columns of Xs and many columns of Os.

The columns of Xs represent 'up-ticks' or buyers, while the Os are 'down-ticks' or sellers.

What's perhaps also evident is that this chart is trending from the lower left-hand section to the upper right-hand section. This is termed an uptrend, and it's designated that way is because frequently following each column of Os (sellers) are a subsequent and higher column of Xs (buyers).

So, after looking at this chart, and someone asks you, "How's the stock market?" You can definitively reply, "It's up and seems to do very well."

Good for you, you just took a big step, so you have an opinion about the market!

Below is a chart of Crude Oil that illustrates what a down-trend looks like.

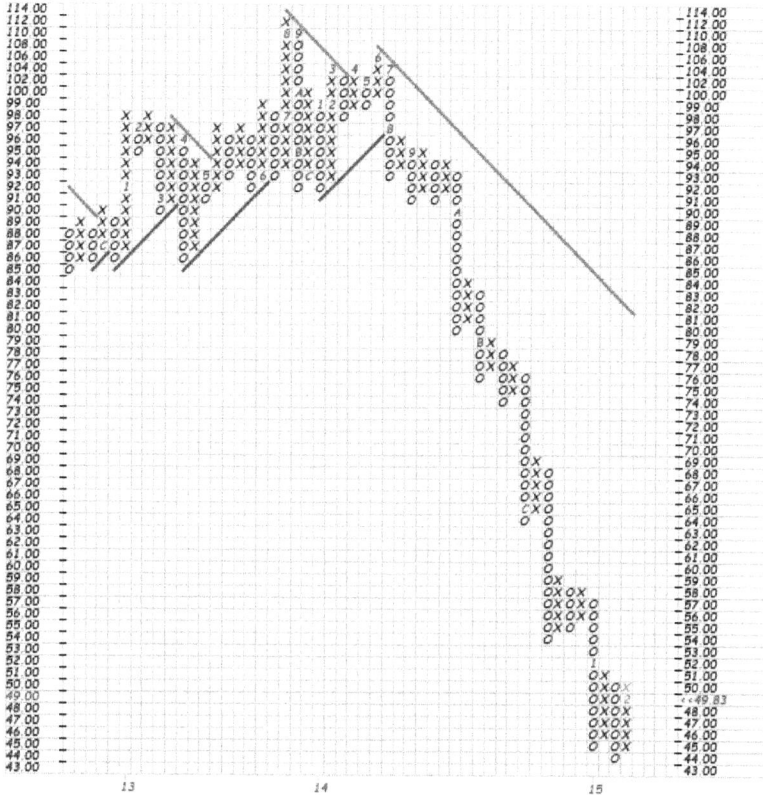

Light Crude Oil - Spot Price (EOD) ($WTIC) CME
02-Feb-2015, 16:00 ET, daily, O: 47.59, H: 50.56, L: 46.67, C: 49.83, V: 496336, Chg: +1.98 (4.14%)
No New P&F Pattern

Traditional, 3 box reversal chart
Bearish Price Obj. (Rev.): Met (78.0)

As you can see, the column of Os is predominant, showing that sellers are prevailing. Again, we need not know why they are selling or that Warren Buffet is one of them; we need only to simply know that there are more sellers than buyers.

So again, when someone asks you what you think

about the Oil Market or what you think about the Energy Market today, you could say, "Well, crude oil has sold off lately and looks like it might take a while before prices move higher."

And you'd be correct! See, you know something about oil and energy!

In both of the above charts, you may have noticed the numbers and letters in some squares. Those represent the months of the year. 1-9 are January through September, and A, B, and C represent October-December (it's only possible to get one digit in each square, thus the letters).

These letters have no impact on the meaning of the chart and are put there only to give you a time reference.

Simple and easy, right? Let's move on.

Finally, Market Movement is at the very foundation of the Law of Supply and Demand.

So, if there's a large supply of something, the price will be lower. If the supply is low, the price will go higher.

When there are more buyers than sellers, prices go up. When there are more sellers than buyers, prices go down. It's as simple as that. Nothing else matters!

And I mean nothing! It's the Law of Supply and Demand! So, what's a Law?

A Law, according to *Wikipedia*, is a system of rules and guidelines which are enforced through social institutions to govern behavior, wherever possible. There are other sets of Laws, called Universal Laws, the Laws of Physics, such as the Law of Gravity or the Law of Relativity.

Universal Laws have always existed, and they were around even before Sir Isaac Newton and Albert Einstein discovered them.

On the subject of quantum physics, I should explain that quantum physicists' only goal is to arrive at one simple conclusion; apples will always fall to the ground. In Einstein's case, he came up with $E=MC^2$.

Hey, I don't want to lose anyone in the left field, so stay with me; there's a point I wish to make! Similarly, Newton's Law of Inertia states, "That every object in a state of uniform motion remains in that state of motion unless an external force applies to it. Markets remain in up-trends (created by buyers buying) until an external force applies to it (sellers selling), creating a reversal in the market called a down-trend.

Again, it's as simple as that!

Nothing we do will change the Laws. Nothing we do alters them. The apple will always fall on our head if we sit under the apple tree with nothing blocking its journey.

You might call it a 'wake up call,' which we could call my work with PNF charts.

Just as the quantum physicist's goal is to arrive at one simple equation, my work is defined by one simple question, "Are buyers in control of a market or are sellers?"

With the knowledge of who is in control of a market, one makes investments aligned in the same direction, up or down.

I explain, clarify, and empower investors to understand the value and implement certain principles while making investment decisions to put them on the correct side or direction of a market.

The method I use shows which markets are going up and which markets are going down. With that evidence and knowledge, investors can see what's happening and need not rely on outside sources for information or opinions. One simple look at a PNF chart and investors can decide which way a market is going.

As an Investment Coach, I educate, coach, encourage, and, therefore, empower those that play 'the Investment Game,' review the Law, and master 'the Investment Game.'

Okay, so now we can conclude that a win in 'The Game' is becoming a 'Successful Investor' and that it wouldn't be a stretch to create 'the Law of Successful Investing.' Right?

Well, I will not take this whole concept to that level; however, there are a few more points regarding the Law of Supply and Demand.

The Law of Supply and Demand states that the price of anything depends upon its availability. Again, if there's a lot of that something available, the price is lower than when there's less of it around. If the price is low, buyers buy. If the price is high, sellers sell.

And our aim is to 'Buy Low, Sell High,' right? Or is it 'Sell High, Buy Low'?

Both statements (Buy Low, Sell High or Sell High, Buy Low), since they're the same, are the basic aim of the Game's strategies.

The problem and the question often become; "How high is high and how low is low?"

What would you do to know, "How high a stock/ETF/Index/commodity/ bond might go?"

What would you do to know, "How low a stock/ETF/Index/commodity/ bond might go?

PNF charts can give investors insights into the answers to those questions since the questions show where there's resistance (when buyers stop buying) and support (where sellers stop selling).

I've said it before, and I'll repeat it, PNF charts are

the perfect pictorial representations of the Law of Supply and Demand, pure and simple. If you'd like more training on PNF charts, you're invited to take my online course called my 'Bootcamp' found at www.theinvestmentcompass.com. During this four-hour online course, I spend a significant amount of time interpreting PNF charts.

As I referenced earlier, if you'd like to look at some PNF charts on your own, go to www.stockcharts.com, the charts there are free. To find a symbol at StockCharts.com, there's an index to locate any stock, ETF, Mutual Fund, or Index that you'd like to view. And next to the symbol box is a drop-down that will show you the Point-and-Figure chart.

I marvel at that 'magic moment' (which I mentioned earlier) because I realize that it occurs in every market and every moment of every day!

For whatever reason(s), the buyer is buying XYZ stock, and at the same precise time, the seller is selling, for whatever reason(s), XYZ stock.

Who Is Correct? Who Is Incorrect?

One has made the investment decision to buy. The other has made the investment decision to sell. Perhaps that explains why we see some confusing headlines and opinions that were discussed earlier.

So, I believe that it's not for me to understand their rationale. I don't have to know what process each went through to come to their exclusive opinions.

My only interest is that they either bought or sold.

I don't have to know 'why' they each made their investment decisions.

A former mentor of mine taught me that the answer to the 'Why' question deserved the cosmic booby prize. "It doesn't matter why," he would say; "it is what is."

It's the simple acceptance of what is, what is happening.

After that, it's only essential for me to learn if other buyers and sellers join the current buyer or seller. When that happens, a trend may be in the making.

Put another way, in the very next moment after the initial trade described above, what happens?

Do other buyers buy (for their independent reasons), or do other sellers sell (for their independent reasons)?

Then there's the next trade, the next, and the next, and the next throughout the day; the process goes on and on.

Each of these trades and the trend (or lack of it) throughout the day becomes important, not the reason they came to the investment decision.

That information, the trend, is what's graphically depicted on the PNF chart.

For centuries, a compass with its four principal points has been used to navigate land and sea. Similarly, I have created what I call the Investment Compass (which is also the name of my LLC), which has eight principal points.

The Principal Points of The Investment Compass (TIC) are eight global markets that will be discussed later. Those eight markets are also the components of the Model Portfolio.

With a clear picture of these eight gigantic markets at your fingertips, you'll have a view of the global economy and its markets enjoyed by very few investors.

These eight markets include US Stocks, US Bonds, Crude Oil, Gold, US Dollar, Foreign Equities, Global Commodities, and US Real Estate. These are massively large markets and will provide investors with an amazing global viewpoint.

What TIC and this system provide you is the basis for making informed investment decisions. You'll learn to recognize when a market, market sector, or an individual stock is going up or going down.

What it looks like when it stops going up, and what it looks like when it starts and continues to go down (knowing up from down). Or, as Kenny Rogers's song goes, "Knowin' when to Hold'em Knowin' when to Fold'em."

You'll learn how it feels to own and have this skill and awareness. The goal is to empower you and give you the confidence that comes with knowing what 'is,' rather than depending on what Wall Street experts say 'is.'

Another clear advantage of the PNF charts is that they 'tell the truth.' They won't tell you what you want to see, which is an important point. Most of us know what we want to happen with an investment, or "if this happens, then my investment will go up," or "like to see _____ (fill in the blank) happen, then my investment would go up."

My advice is the same given by Crash Davis (played by Kevin Costner), a seasoned catcher, hired to coach an up-and-coming young pitcher, 'Nuke' LaLoosh (played by Tim Robbins) in the movie 'Bull Durham' "Don't think, Meat!"

I'm serious; one of my biggest challenges as an investor is staying out of the way, accepting what's happening in a market, and reacting accordingly rather than 'presupposing' what I want it to be.

There's no better feeling to have during investing than knowing 'what', rather than 'why', as you use the PNF charts of the eight principal markets of the Investment Compass and other investments.

Chapter 6
The Teeter Totter Principle

Now, let's go over The Teeter Totter Principle (TTP) again.

It is my creation; it goes like this. You all know how a teeter totter works; one side goes up while the other goes down and vice versa, assuming an imbalance with the weight on each two.

Well, with ETFs, the same is usually true.

When the PNF chart of an ETF goes up, the PNF chart of the Inverse ETF goes down, and when the PNF chart of the Inverse ETF goes up, the PNF chart of the ETF goes down.

However, I discovered with trial-and-error that this Principal is not always true with investments. That is why I added the third component, the Index, not just considering the ETF and the Inverse ETF.

Here is how it works.

If the PNF chart of the Index is going up, and there is congruency, it should follow that when the PNF chart of the ETF will go up, and the PNF chart of the Inverse ETF should go down.

If that is **not the case** and at least **one of the three** is not behaving like a teeter totter, there is no "signal" or reversal in any position. The Teeter Totter Principle requires all three (the Index, the ETF, and the Inverse ETF) PNF charts to agree on the direction of the markets we are considering.

What is essential for you to know is that we, as investors, cannot own an Index; we can only buy the ETF or the Inverse ETF. And you might be surprised to learn that the Index's chart does not always mirror the chart of ETF.

Let's go through some examples, and I think you will get the hang of it.

The first market we'll look at is the Gold Market. Here is the PNF Chart of the Gold Index on the last day of May 2019:

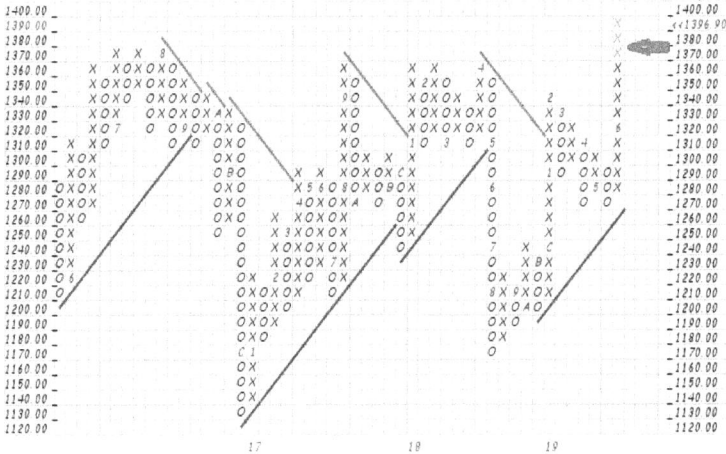

$GOLD Gold - Continuous Contract (EOD) CME
20-Jun-2019, 14:30 ET, daily, O: 1,364.50, H: 1,397.70, L: 1,361.30, C: 1,396.90, V: 51407000, Chg: +48.10 (3.57%)
P&F Pattern Double Top Breakout on 31-May-2019
Scaling: Traditional [Reversal: 3]

This shows that at the actual time (June 20, 2019), buyers took the Gold Index price over the top diagonal lines (resistance lines) and above the bottom solid resistance lines established at 1370 over the previous three years.

This signed a potential change toward the Gold Market.

Since, as I pointed out earlier, we can't buy the Index, we turn to the ETF which we can buy GLD, the ETF of that Index:

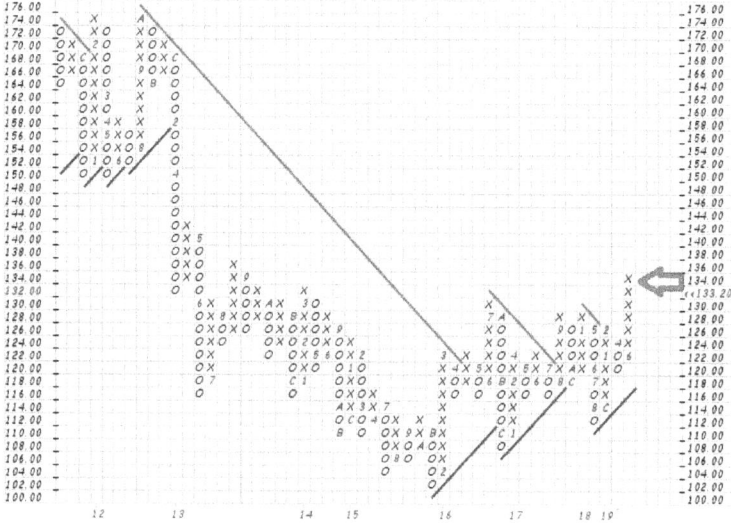

GLD SPDR Gold Shares NYSE
28-Jun-2019, 16:00 ET, daily, O: 133.05, H: 133.34, L: 132.61, C: 133.20, V: 8076966, Chg: +0.36 (0.27%)
P&F Pattern: Spread Triple Top Breakout on 20-Jun-2019
Scaling: Traditional [Reversal: 3]

Note that the "signal," or what is called a "break-out," we saw with the Index, roughly a week sooner, we see the same "signal" we got with GLD.

However, now we have an agreement between the Index and the ETF.

Next, we turn to the Inverse ETF of the Gold Market, GLL, to see if it goes in the opposite direction:

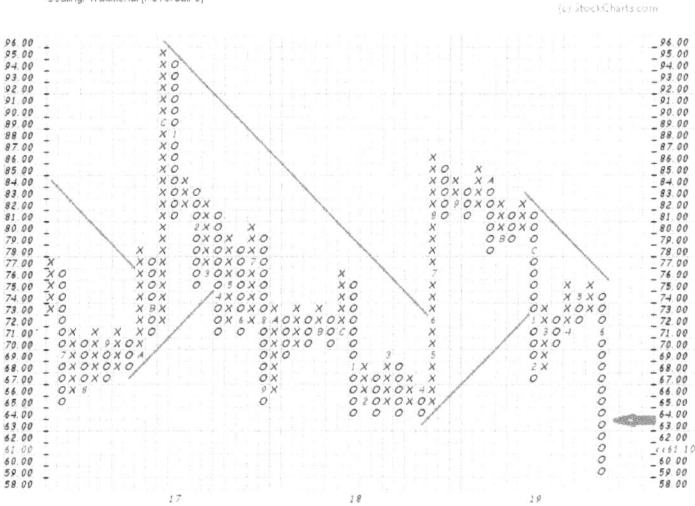

GLL ProShares UltraShort Gold NYSE
28-Jun-2019, 16:00 ET, daily, O: 61.15, H: 61.56, L: 60.99, C: 61.10, V: 25288, Chg: -0.229 (-0.37%)
P&F Pattern: Double Bottom Breakdown on 03-Jun-2019
Scaling: Traditional [Reversal: 3]

Bingo! Right on, cue!

We have confirmation of a change toward the Gold Market!

The Teeter Totter Principle confirms. gold is going higher! The ETF went up, and the Inverse ETF broke down.

First, we had the Index penetrate support. Second, the ETF did the same thing. And third, the Inverse ETF confirmed that gold was going higher in price by breaking below the strong support (going back to 2016) at forty-five.

This is the confirmation I look for, all three to agree on the Gold Market's direction.

Remember, the ETF and the Inverse ETF go in opposite directions.

Just like a teeter totter, when one side goes down, because of more weight, the other side goes up, and when one side goes up, the other side goes down.

A teeter totter can't do anything else when there is an imbalance and, as we see in the PNF chart below of August 31 (a month later), GLD continued higher:

GLD SPDR Gold Shares NYSE
30-Aug-2019, 16:00 ET, daily, O: 143.84, H: 144.882, L: 143.02, C: 143.75, V: 9614418, Chg: -0.37 (-0.26%)
P&F Pattern Spread Triple Top Breakout on 20-Jun-2019
Scaling: Traditional [Reversal: 3]

The other analogy I like to use is how water moves on the inland surface of the Earth.

If you imagine each of the components of my methodology, the Index, the ETF, and the Inverse ETF, as small streams, each of them will meander in their respective directions.

They are each moving to their destination.

Eventually, they merge and form one stream of water, and they are then a more powerful force because of the increase in the volume of water.

Likewise, the Index, the ETF, and the Inverse ETF combine to create a more powerful force.

That is where this analogy ends.

And yet, another analogy gives us another visual.

This new analogy is also about water; however, this analogy is about how to tide water's work.

Unlike streams and rivers, tides bring water in, and tides bring water out; that is why all ships in the harbor go up when the tide comes in and why they go down when the tide goes out.

The water changes directions from coming into going out.

And, like tides, markets change directions. Sometimes they go up, and sometimes they go down; however, not with tides regularity.

This methodology I am describing not only gives you a signal of the potentiality of trends in the marketplace, but it also gives you a sign when those changes are happening.

Let me show you another market that offers how this methodology signals a change in the Real Estate Market.

Again, using the same sequence of looking at the perfect pictorial representation of The Law of Supply and Demand the PNF charts, the Index, the ETF, and the Inverse ETF.

First, the Real Estate Index:

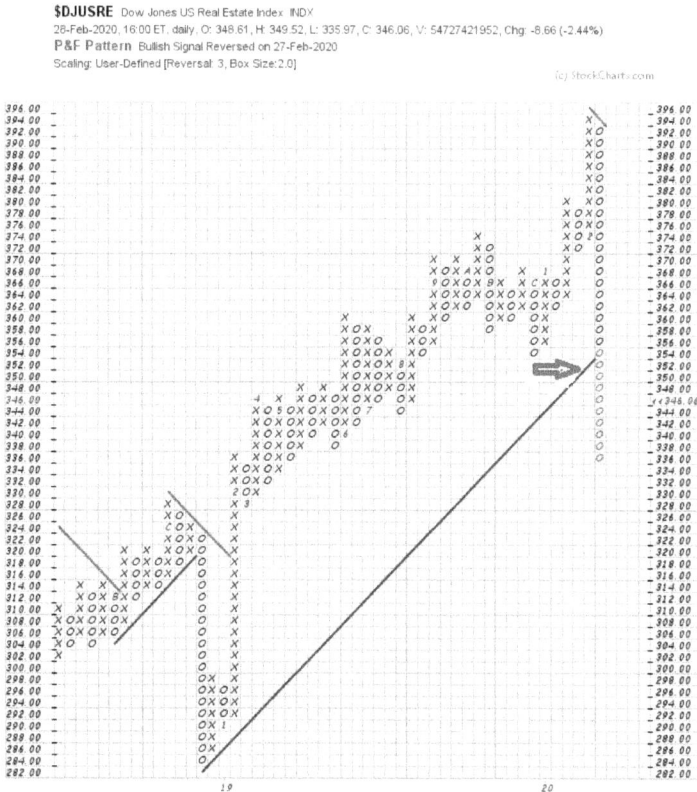

$DJUSRE Dow Jones US Real Estate Index INDX
28-Feb-2020, 16:00 ET, daily, O: 348.61, H: 349.52, L: 335.97, C: 346.06, V: 54727421952, Chg: -8.66 (-2.44%)
P&F Pattern Bullish Signal Reversed on 27-Feb-2020
Scaling: User-Defined [Reversal: 3, Box Size:2.0]

The Real Estate Market has been in a significant uptrend for several years; however, as this chart shows, sellers took this market below a major support level when the price penetrated the blue support line, as pointed out above by the arrow and previous support column of Os at 354.

On that same day, VNQ, the symbol for the Real Estate ETF, looked like this:

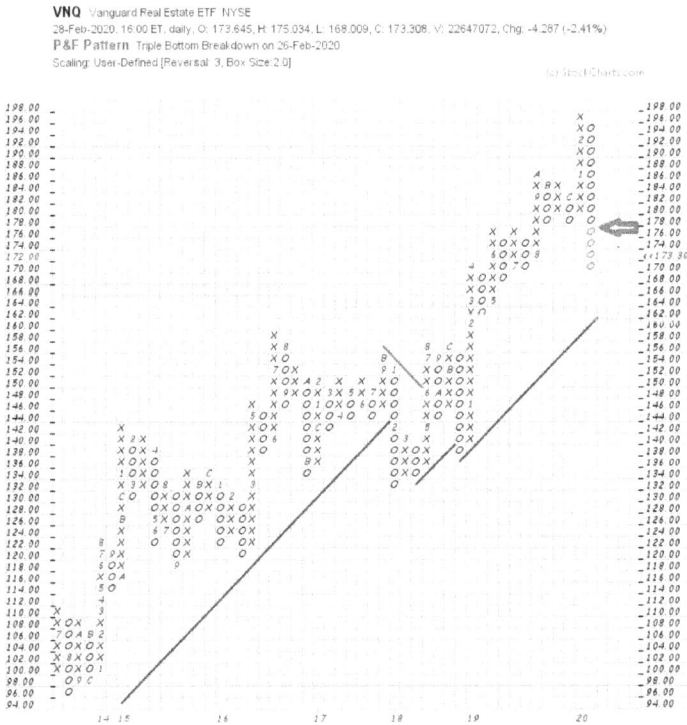

VNQ Vanguard Real Estate ETF NYSE
28-Feb-2020, 16:00 ET, daily, O: 173.645, H: 175.034, L: 168.009, C: 173.308, V: 22647072, Chg: -4.287 (-2.41%)
P&F Pattern Triple Bottom Breakdown on 26-Feb-2020
Scaling: User-Defined [Reversal: 3, Box Size: 2.0]

Okay, both the Index and the ETF are giving me the initial signs of a reversal or a "sell" signal in the Real Estate market.

To confirm, we look at the Inverse ETF, SRS to see if the "teeter tottered."

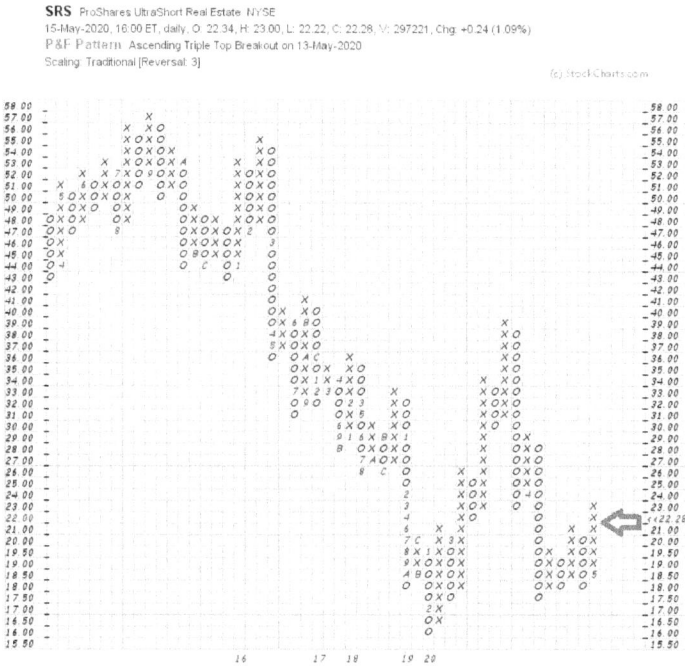

SRS ProShares UltraShort Real Estate NYSE
15-May-2020, 16:00 ET, daily, O: 22.34, H: 23.00, L: 22.22, C: 22.28, V: 297221, Chg: +0.24 (1.09%)
P&F Pattern: Ascending Triple Top Breakout on 13-May-2020
Scaling: Traditional [Reversal: 3]

Yes, the Teeter Totter Principle worked again!

When the ETF, VNQ, goes down, the Inverse ETF, SRS, **should g**o up if there is an actual reversal in the Real Estate Market. The "agreement" amongst these three PNF charts of the Index, the ETF, and the Inverse ETF confirms, with this methodology, that Real Estate is reversing to the downside and signals that the investor is directed to the Inverse ETF, SRS.

Now that you have seen which direction of two markets, Gold and Real Estate, I will turn to the one that so many investors are interested in the Bond Market.

This is an example of a market that has been on a twenty-year bull run.

Twenty years!

Buyers have dominated this market more clearly than any I have ever seen. It is a fantastic chart.

As usual, we begin with a look at the PNF chart of the Bond Index.

$USB CME CBOT 30-Year US Treasury Bond Price (EOD) INDX
19-May-2020, 16:00 ET, daily, O: 177.531, H: 177.531, L: 177.531, C: 177.531, Chg: +0.396 (0.22%)
No recent chart pattern found
Scaling: Traditional [Reversal: 3]

A look at the Bond ETF, TLT, to see if it agrees with the chart of the Index and buyers' domination provides a lot of detailed information and should not be overlooked.

Sure, there are columns of Os; however, they are relatively short-lived, and the price always remained above the blue support line.

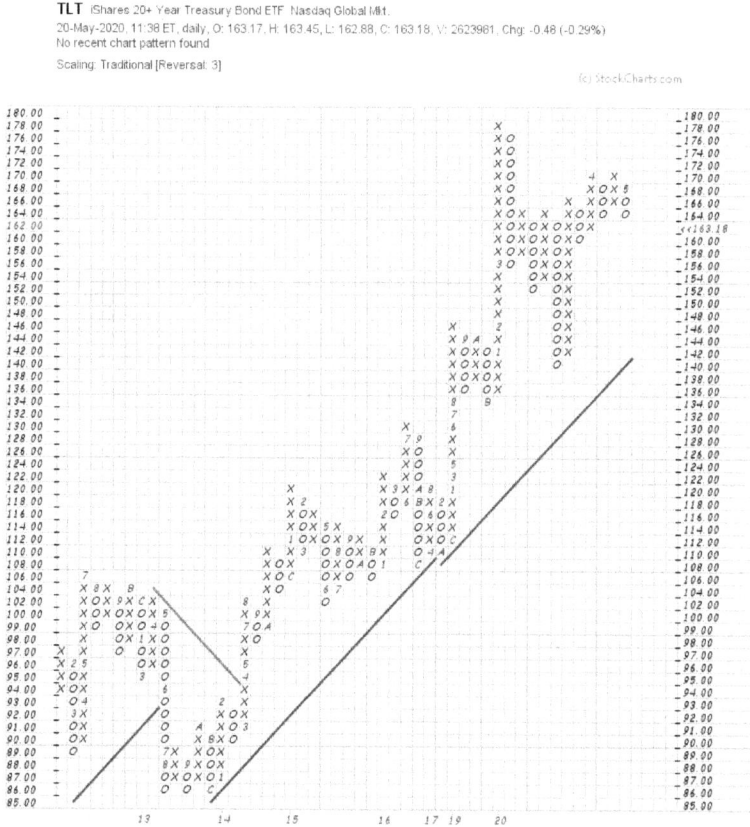

TLT iShares 20+ Year Treasury Bond ETF Nasdaq Global Mkt.
20-May-2020, 11:38 ET, daily, O: 163.17, H: 163.45, L: 162.88, C: 163.18, V: 2623981, Chg: -0.48 (-0.29%)
No recent chart pattern found

Scaling: Traditional [Reversal: 3]

And the following chart of the Inverse ETF, TBT, confirms our position in Bonds and, again, showing The Teeter Totter Principle.

```
TBT ProShares UltraShort 20+ Year Treasury NYSE
01-May-2020, 16:00 ET, daily, O: 15.53, H: 15.70, L: 15.39, C: 15.47, V: 1469712, Chg: -0.21 (-1.34%)
P&F Pattern Double Bottom Breakdown on 19-Mar-2020
Scaling: Traditional [Reversal: 3]
                                                                    (c) StockCharts.com

78.00  X                                                                     78.00
77.00  X 1                                                                   77.00
76.00  C O                                                                   76.00
75.00  O                                                                     75.00
74.00  O                                                                     74.00
73.00  O                                                                     73.00
72.00  O                                                                     72.00
71.00  O                                                                     71.00
70.00  O X                                                                   70.00
69.00  O X O X                                                               69.00
68.00  O X O X O                                                             68.00
67.00  2 X O X O X                                                           67.00
66.00  O  3   O X O                                                          66.00
65.00         O 4 O                                                          65.00
64.00         O   O                                                          64.00
63.00             O                                                          63.00
62.00             O                                                          62.00
61.00       5 X                                                              61.00
60.00       O X 7                                                            60.00
59.00       O 6 O                                                            59.00
58.00       O   O X                                                          58.00
57.00           O X O                                                        57.00
56.00           O X O                                                        56.00
55.00           8 X O                                                        55.00
54.00           O 9 O                                                        54.00
53.00           O   A                                                        53.00
52.00           O                                                            52.00
51.00         O X                                                            51.00
50.00         O X C         X                                                50.00
49.00         O X O         X 7 X                                            49.00
48.00         O X O     X   X O X O                                          48.00
47.00         O X O X   X O X O X O                                          47.00
46.00         O X O X 1 X   X O 6 O                                          46.00
45.00         O   O X O 3 0 5 O   O 9   X                                    45.00
44.00           O   O X O X       O X O X C                                  44.00
43.00             O X O X       8 X O X O                                    43.00
42.00             O X O X       O X O 9 O                                    42.00
41.00             O X O 4       O X A   O                                    41.00
40.00             O X O         O     C 1 X         X                        40.00
39.00             O X           O     X O X 4       X C                      39.00
38.00             O 2           O     X O 3 O   X   X X O                    38.00
37.00             O             2 X   X O   O   X 3 X 5 X O                  37.00
36.00                           O X 6 X   O X   2 O 4 O A O                  36.00
35.00                           O 3 O X   6 X 8 X   X O   O                  35.00
34.00                           O   O B   O 7 O X C X   O                    34.00
33.00                               O A   O   O A O 1       1                33.00
32.00                               O X       9   O         3                32.00
31.00                               O X                     5                31.00
30.00                               7 9                     O                30.00
29.00                               O                       7                29.00
28.00                                                       8 8              28.00
27.00                                                       O X 1            27.00
26.00                                                       O X O            26.00
25.00                                                       O 8 O            25.00
24.00                                                       O   O            24.00
23.00                                                       2                23.00
22.00                                                       O                22.00
21.00                                                       O     X          21.00
20.00                                                       O     X O        20.00
19.50                                                       3     X O        19.50
19.00                                                       O X   X O        19.00
18.50                                                       O X O X O        18.50
18.00                                                       O X O X O        18.00
17.50                                                       O X O X O        17.50
17.00                                                       O X O X O        17.00
16.50                                                       O X O. O         16.50
16.00                                                       O X   O          16.00
15.50                                                       O X   O          15.50
15.00                                                       O X   4   <c15.47 15.00
14.50                                                       O               14.50
14.00                                                                        14.00
        14            15           16   17        18      19 20
```

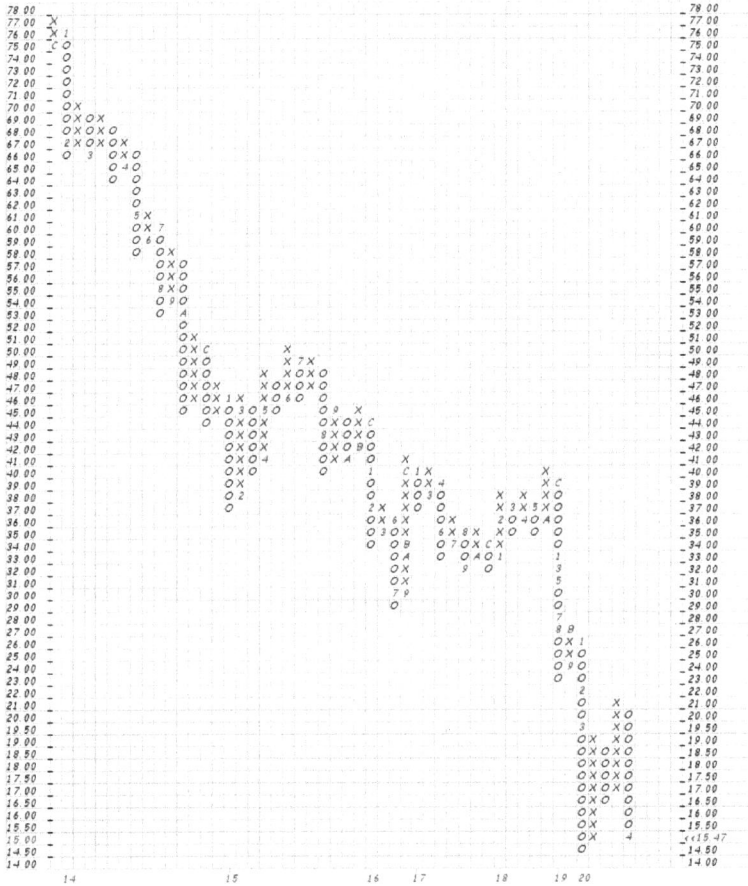

TLT goes up, and TBT goes down just like a Teeter Totter!

The Bond Sector has never, in the last twenty years, signaling a reversal in its uptrend, and during these years, investors would have gained confidence in their Bond position and be at ease by staying in this sector as the PNF charts verified the uptrend.

During my long career, I have never seen buyers dominate a market for such an extended period, as has been the case with Bonds.

The next market I want to show you is similar, however, not as conclusive as to the Bond Market: the US Stock Market. Here is the S&P Index PNF chart.

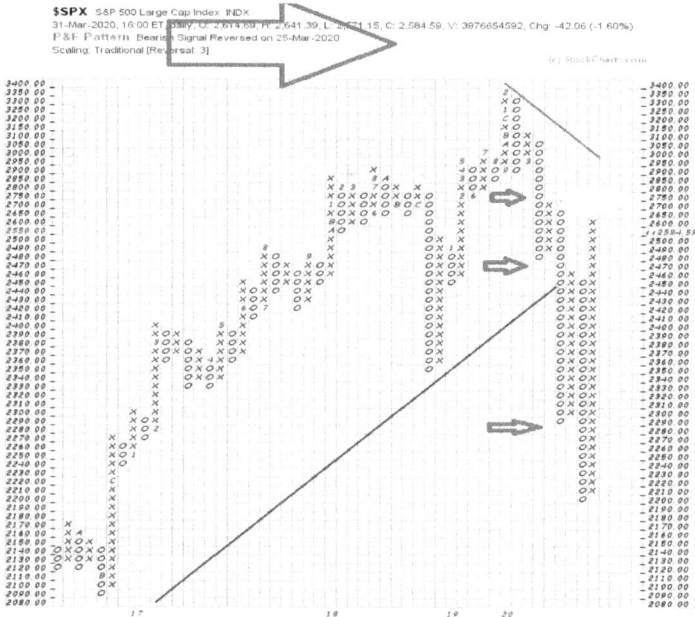

The uptrend is evident from 2016 but also shows several interruptions of the buyer's dominance that has taken place in more recent times.

Three times on March 3, 2020, sellers broke below support levels. Those events demanded looking at the ETF, SPY since it, like the Bond Market, it has been in an uptrend since 2009. Here is the PNF chart of the ETF, SPY:

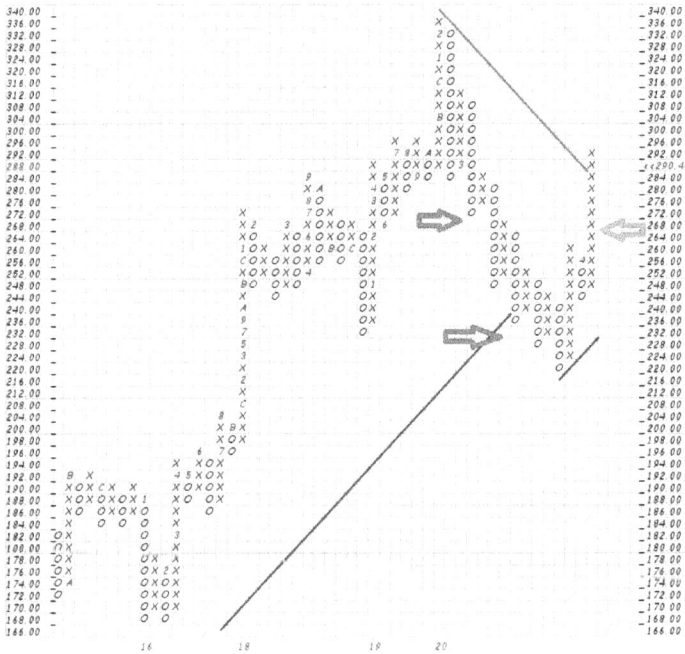

SPY SPDR S&P 500 ETF NYSE
30-Apr-2020, 16:00 ET, daily, O: 291.71, H: 293.324, L: 288.59, C: 290.48, V: 122892320, Chg: -2.73 (-0.93%)
P&F Pattern: Double Top Breakout on 06-Apr-2020
Scaling: Traditional [Reversal: 3]

The two right facing arrows show where sellers took SPY through several support levels, followed by the buyers returning to the market, bringing the price beyond resistance levels (note left facing arrow).

Is this the beginning of a bear market or the resumption of the bull market?

That is the big question at present. The interesting thing is that the answer may have already been revealed by reading this book.

Since we haven't determined or confirmed the US Stock Market's change of direction, we look at the Inverse ETF, SH, to see if there is any additional information that will help us with an answer to our question.

This is a long chart and needs the whole next page.

SH ProShares Short S&P500 NYSE
20-May-2020, 12:09 ET, daily, O: 23.65, H: 23.668, L: 23.48, C: 23.515, V: 5146053, Chg: -0.455 (-1.90%)
No recent chart pattern found

Scaling: Traditional [Reversal: 3]

(c) StockCharts.com

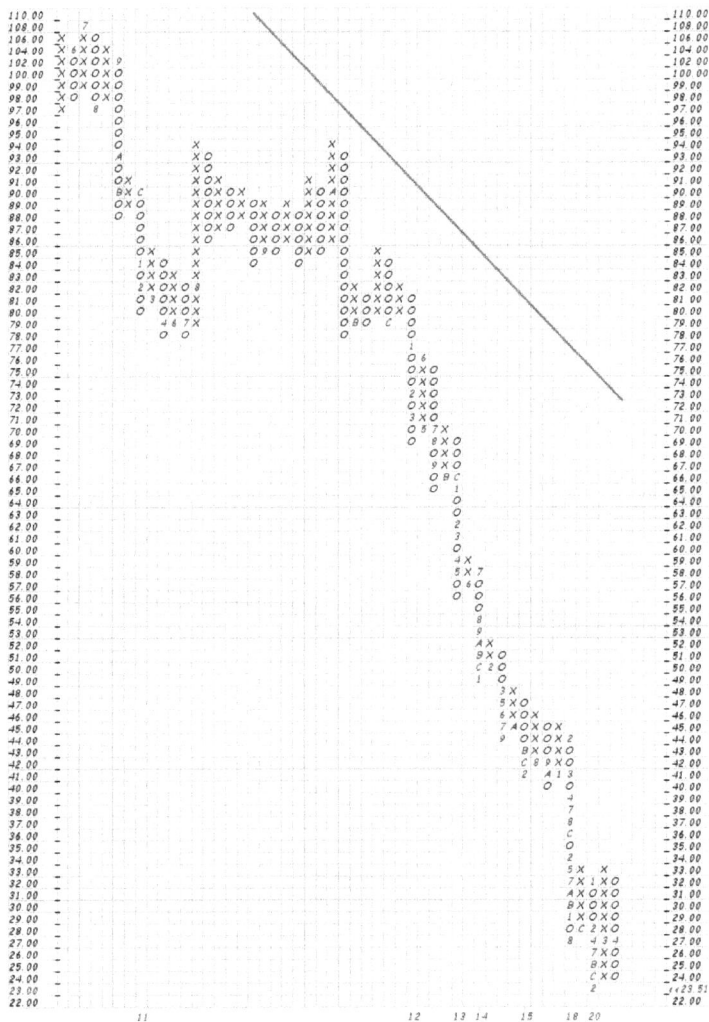

Sellers continue to dominate SH since 2012, so the uptrend stays in effect!

When analyzing the three charts, there is agreement on whether the US Stock Market reverses its direction?

The answer is NO. There are no buyers in SH, the Inverse ETF, and no sellers of SPY.

Until buyers take SH over the resistance at 33 and sellers dominate the Index and SPY charts, my position is to remain in SPY.

The teeter keeps tottering!

There cannot be a reversal down in SPY until there is a reversal upward and goes above resistance in SH, The Teeter Totter Principle!

It should be clear by now that this methodology is not a trading technique. It is a plan for the long-term investor that wants to be sure that she/he is on the "right" side of the market.

I am never concerned about which direction a market is going; I am only concerned about being sure that I am following the dominant force's direction, either the buyers or the sellers. They are who move markets up or down!

There is one market; however, that has been very volatile in 2020, the Crude Oil Sector.

The PNF chart of the Crude Oil Index follows:

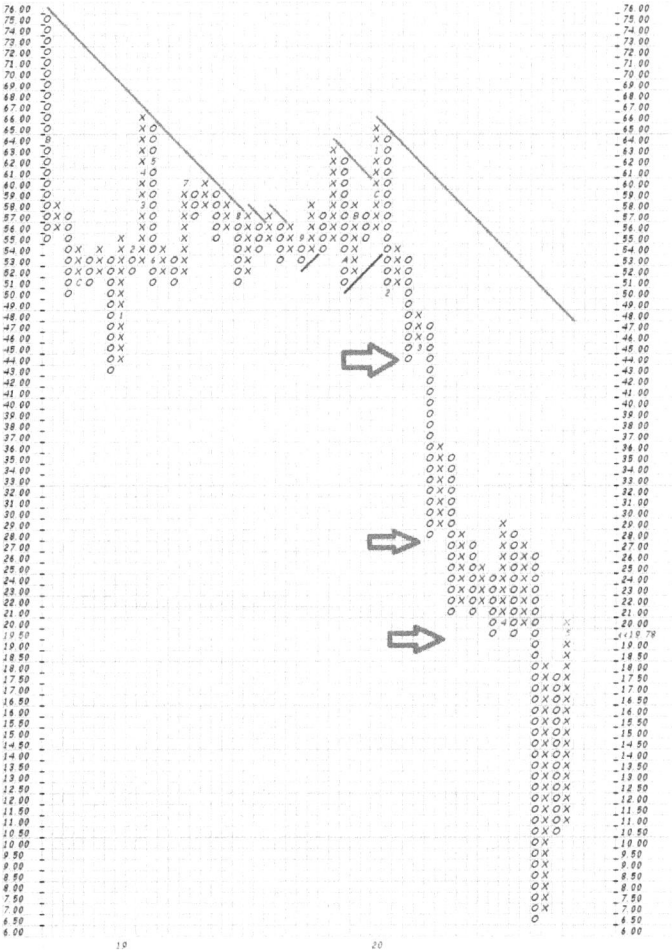

$WTIC Light Crude Oil - Continuous Contract (EOD) CME
01-May-2020, 16:00 ET, daily, O: 19.04, H: 20.48, L: 18.07, C: 19.78, V: 39456600, Chg: +0.94 (4.99%)
P&F Pattern: Double Top Breakout on 30-Apr-2020
Scaling: Traditional [Reversal: 3]

The initial breakdown in Crude was early in March 2020 at the first arrow in the chart above and where the price broke below the support at 43 back in 2018.

Meanwhile, this is what the Oil ETF, UCO (distorted because it is such a large chart) looked like this:

Straight down!

The Inverse ETF, SCO, below, was also volatile after it broke out above resistance (red arrow) on March 20:

SCO ProShares UltraShort Bloomberg Crude Oil NYSE
01-May-2020, 16:00 ET, daily, O: 48.45, H: 50.70, L: 46.88, C: 48.76, V: 5306875, Chg: +2.20 (4.73%)
No recent chart pattern found

Scaling: Traditional [Reversal: 3]

(c) StockCharts.com

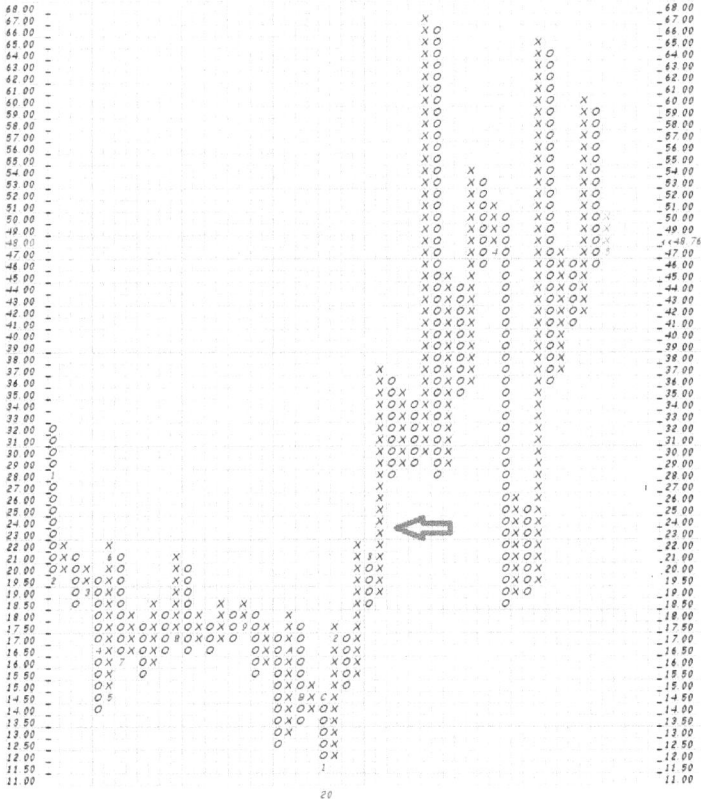

Even though the price went back down, it reached support just below 20 and has gone back up since then.

This is confirmation, although volatile, and is evidence that the downtrend in Crude is probably, but not certainly, over.

Another sector in the marketplace with all four of the ingredients for my methodology (1. A vast market.

2. An Index. 3. An ETF. And 4. An Inverse ETF) are Foreign Equities. The Index I use for this sector of the marketplace is the Morgan Stanley EAFA (Europe, Australia, and the Far East) Index.

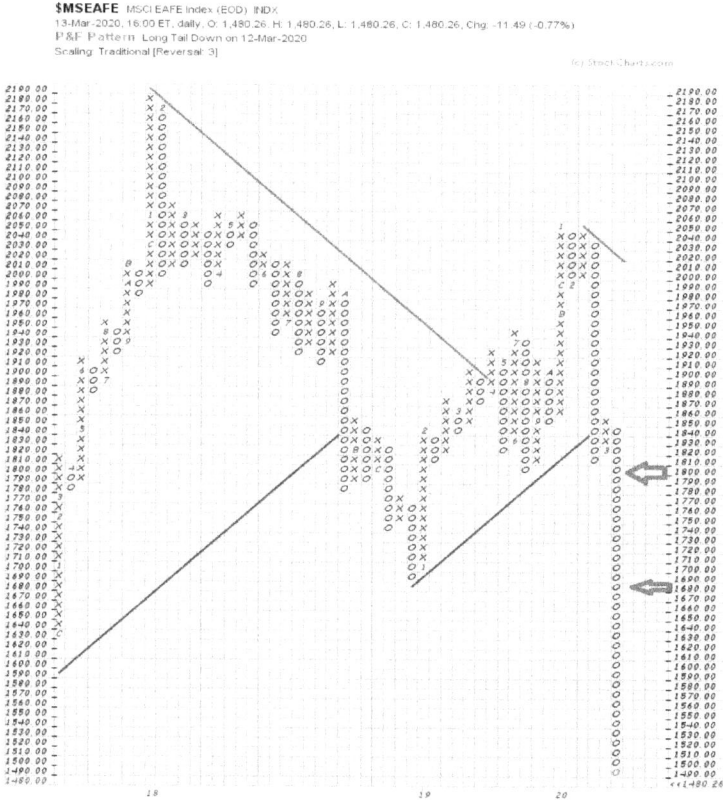

This market also suffered COVID-19 in March 2020 and broke support at two levels. See arrows.

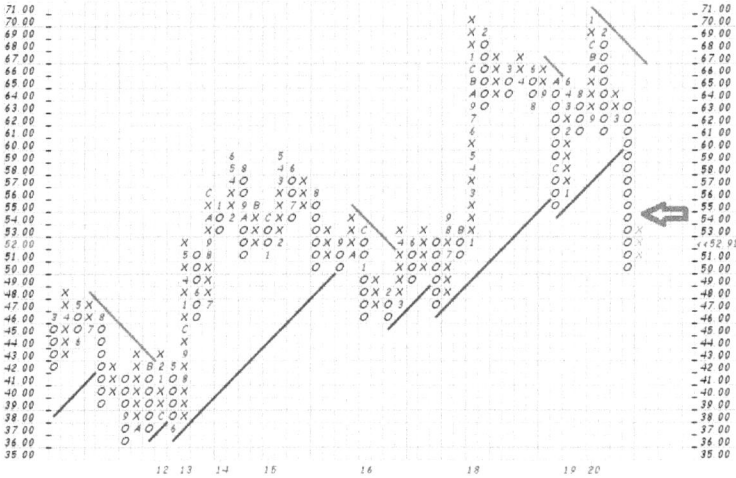

EFA (iShares MSCI EAFE ETF NYSE
13-Mar-2020, 16:00 ET, daily, O: 53.12, H: 53.30, L: 49.77, C: 52.91, V: 73544648, Chg: +3.02 (6.05%)
No recent chart pattern found

Scaling: Traditional [Reversal: 3]

(c) StockCharts.com

On the same day, the ETF, EFA, also broke below the support (showed by the blue support line) and agreed with the Foreign Equity Index chart.

Then, one day later, the Inverse ETF, EFU followed suit, confirming the change in the price's direction of Foreign Equities to a downtrend:

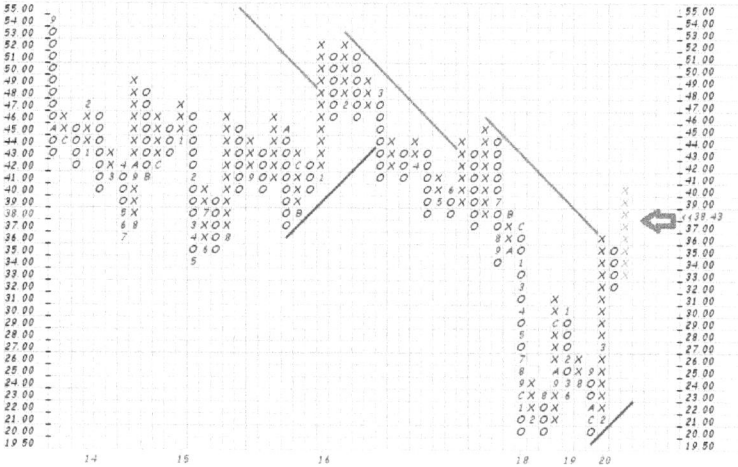

EFU ProShares UltraShort MSCI EAFE NYSE
16-Mar-2020, 16:00 ET, daily, O: 39.09, H: 40.08, L: 36.691, C: 38.439, V: 8158, Chg: +4.271 (12.50%)
P&F Pattern Double Top Breakout on 16-Mar-2020
Scaling: Traditional [Reversal: 3]

We have an agreement! Foreign Equities have given me a signal that they are going lower and that I should be in the Inverse ETF, EFU.

Once again, The Teeter Totter Law is displayed in plain sight!

Now I want to cover the US Dollar sector with the chart of the Index, first on the next page:

$USD US Dollar Index - Cash Settle (EOD) ICE
21-May-2020, 16:00 ET, daily, O: 99.18, H: 99.54, L: 99.03, C: 99.403, Chg: +0.268 (0.27%)
P&F Pattern: Double Top Breakout on 17-Mar-2020
Scaling: Traditional [Reversal: 3]

(c) StockCharts.com

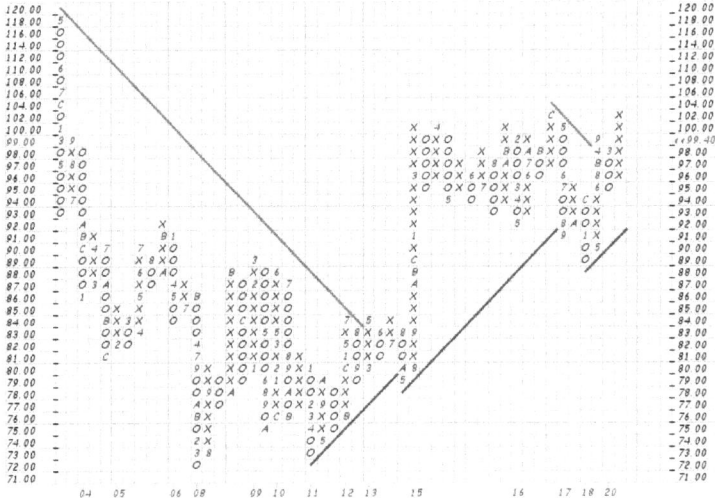

The US Dollar has been in a trading range for over four years. It has been trading between 89, on the low end of the range, and 102 at the high end.

Basically, since 2015 it has been dominated by the buyers.

A look at the ETF, UUP, is where we check next:

UUP Invesco DB US Dollar Index Bullish Fund NYSE
22-May-2020, 13:47 ET, daily, O: 2,700.00, H: 2,703.00, L: 2,698.00, C: 2,701.50, V: 1464219, Chg: +10.50 (0.39%)
No recent chart pattern found

Scaling: Traditional [Reversal: 3]

(c) StockCharts.com

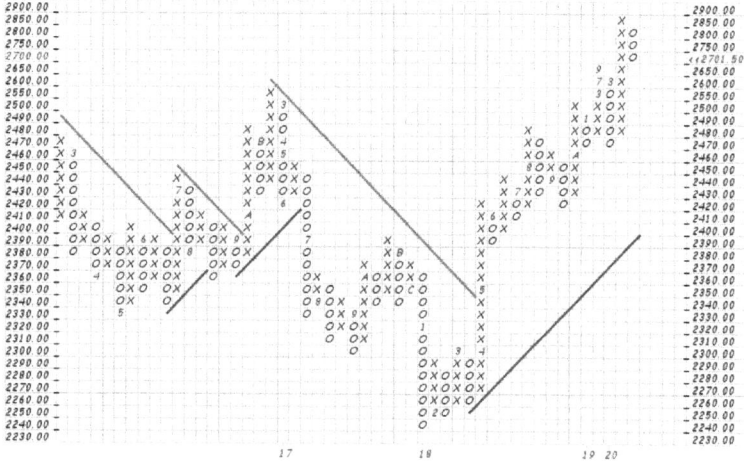

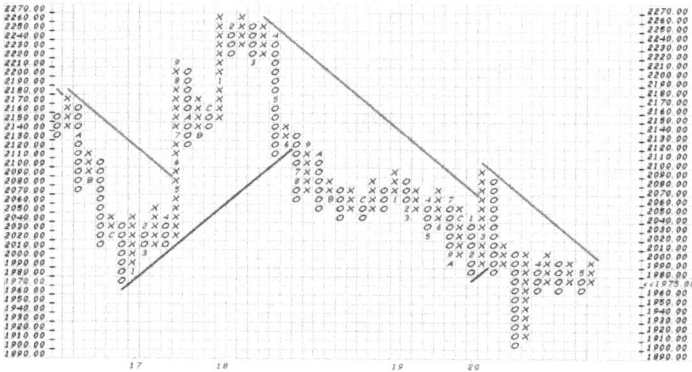

The ETF, UUP, agrees with the Index's chart. The US Dollar is going higher.

So, the next step is to look at the chart of the Inverse ETF, UDN:

UDN Invesco DB US Dollar Index Bearish Fund NYSE
22-May-2020, 13:38 ET, daily, O: 1,978.00, H: 1,978.00, L: 1,975.00, C: 1,975.00, V: 6938, Chg: -8.00 (-0.40%)
No recent chart pattern found

Scaling: Traditional [Reversal: 3]

(c) StockCharts.com

Since all three charts agree, the methodology suggests investing in the ETF, UPP, until a reversal occurs.

There you have it, an outline using various markets and applying my methodology.

In each of the seven markets we covered, there are four characteristics that each has:

- ✓ They are vast markets, great liquidity.
- ✓ They each have an Index and a PNF chart of the Index.
- ✓ They each have an ETF and a PNF chart of the ETF.
- ✓ They each have an Inverse ETF and a PNF chart of the Inverse ETF.

When all three of the PNF charts agree as to the direction, up or down, then the appropriate ETF can be purchased with high confidence.

The Teeter Totter Principle helps to strengthen the position you are taking. If one of the ETFs is going up, the other must go down, and if one of the ETFs is going down, the other must go up, strengthening your decision.

Once you have determined which ETF represents the direction, you think the market is going; you stay with that position until it shows a reversal (that the teeter totter is going in the opposite direction).

The biggest challenge for investors using this methodology is discovering when an uptrend turns into a downtrend or when a downtrend turns into an uptrend.

These transitions (from down to up and up to down) are sometimes not so obvious. And it is during those transitions that investors must pay close attention to what **all three** of the three charts are telling you.

That is the reason I use three charts. There must be an agreement with **all three**.

Pay attention to the charts, not what you "think or want" to happen. Wishful thinking does not work!

Don't ask, "Why?" A market or ETF is doing what it is doing. Accept the evidence and rely on The Law of Supply and Demand.

Again, my mentor taught me that the answer to the "Why?" deserves the cosmic booby prize, "It doesn't matter why," he would say, "because that is the way it is; the reason "Why? It doesn't matter!"

The methodology that I have shared with you has been evolving in my mind for many years. I wanted to develop these simple steps so that anyone could understand what is going on with a market and that the process is logical and makes sense.

If you are an investor, that would like to analyze an individual stock, let me give you two examples of how you can still use a PNF chart to guide your investment decision because I still believe that **every** investment decision should begin by **first** looking at the PNF chart of that investment vehicle.

On the next page is the PNF chart of Microsoft.

Whether you own MSFT and are looking for a level to get out or are looking to buy MSFT, this how to start your analysis and benefit from the PNF chart's power.

MSFT Microsoft Corp. Nasdaq Global Select Mkt.
22-May-2020, 16:00 ET, daily, O: 183.19, H: 184.46, L: 182.54, C: 183.51, V: 20826898, Chg: +0.08 (0.04%)
No recent chart pattern found

Scaling: Traditional [Reversal: 3]

(c) StockCharts.com

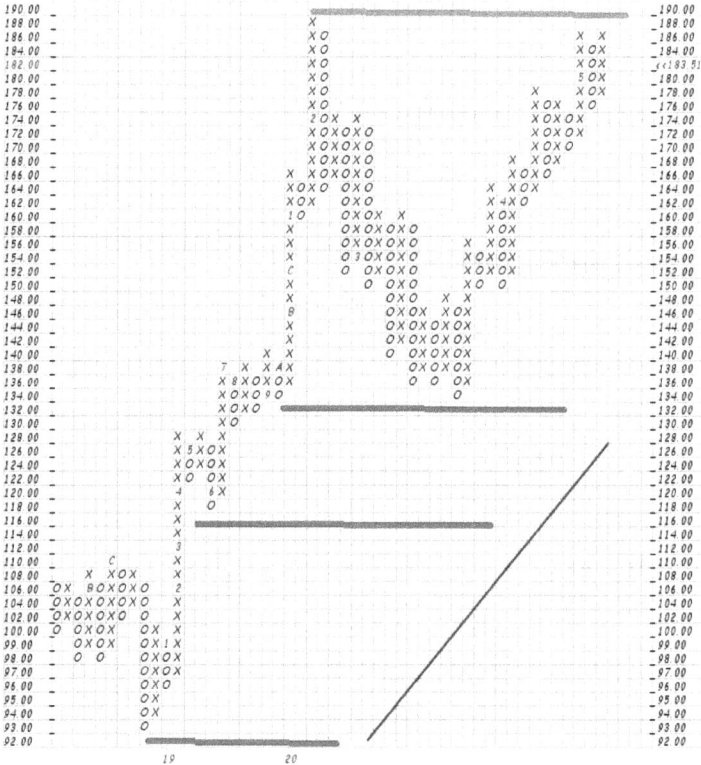

Above you will see three horizontal lines at the bottom (support level) and a slanted line (resistance level) that I have placed on the chart.

This tells you that buyers have entered the market near or at the second horizontal support line in the past, and sellers entered the market at or near the top resistance line. (Make sure you see and understand these lines.)

We learn from this "road map" that if the price of MSFT ever penetrated the bottom line, one would expect it to go to the second from the bottom line, and if that was penetrated, it could next attract buyers at the third to the bottom line. The rationale is that buyers have paid that price in the past and are likely to do it again.

If buyers took the price above the top resistance line, it would likely go higher, and since that line represents an all-time high, buyers will keep buying until sellers enter the game and take it lower.

When a new high is printed, the process begins all over again.

The point is, if you already own MSFT, you must like the company, and now the question is one of, at what price?

If you do not own MSFT and you want to buy it, it must mean that you like the company, and it still becomes a question of, at what price?

Therein lies the value of the PNF chart!

Here is another example of using the PNF chart of a company in a different industry. On the chart is the PNF of Exxon in the energy sector:

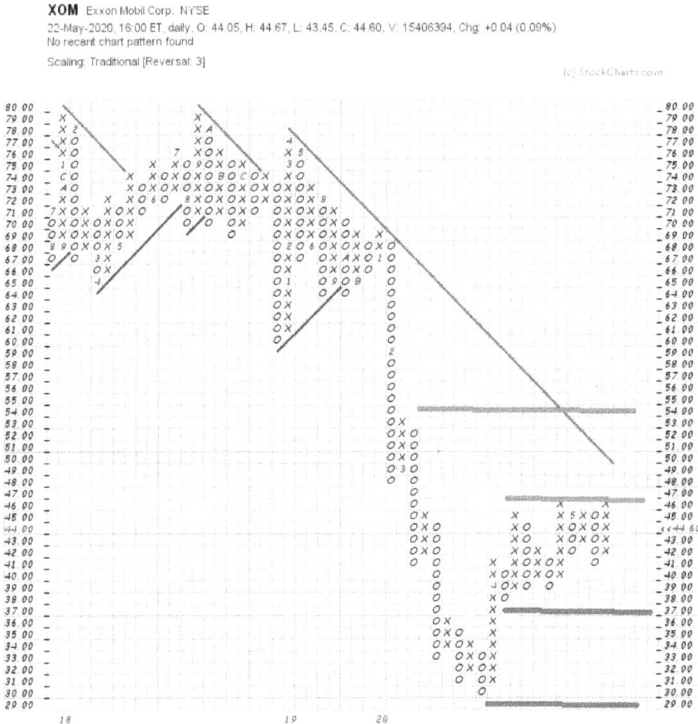

Overall, we see that XOM has been in a downtrend for over four years.

Next, we can see that most recently, buyers have bought.

First buyers came into XON after it printed thirty on the chart above. Then, after a short sell-off, they bid the price up to the top horizontal line resistance point, and sellers took the price down to the support line (third horizontal line), which is exactly where buyers, once again, took the price back up to the second horizontal line (three times!).

That brings us to where the price is on May 22, 2020.

So, the question now is. Will buyers take it even higher, or will sellers take it lower?

If you own XOM, you like the company and will want to know where there support and where there is resistance. Additionally, you will want to have this information if you are looking to purchase XOM.

You now have a roadmap to guide you as you decide where there is support and where there is resistance.

Or, put another way, where there is supply and where there is demand.

It's all as simple as that!

Chapter 7
Another PNF Tool – The Bullish Percent Chart

So, what is the Bullish Percentage?

The S&P 500 Bullish Percent Index, for example, is a point-and-figure chart that derives its value from the point-and-figure charts of the 500 stocks that comprise the S&P 500.

Here is how it works:

> ➢ If an increasing number of those 500 stocks show buy signals on their point-and-figure charts, the S&P 500 Bullish Percent Index will move higher.
> ➢ If an increasing number of those 500 stocks show sell signals on their point-and-figure charts, the S&P 500

Bullish Percent Index will
move lower.

Bullish Percent of Charts are enormously powerful. Unfortunately, there are limitations, and you need to be clear on this point.

You <u>may not</u> find a Bullish Percent Chart for every investment vehicle that you may consider. However, it is a significant starting point, particularly for most Sectors of the market.

Below is a list of the Sectors:

DJIA Bullish Percent Index ($BPINDU)

DJTA Bullish Percent Index ($BPTRAN)

Gold Miners Bullish Percent Index ($BPGDM)

Nasdaq 100 Bullish Percent Index ($BPNDX)

Nasdaq Composite Bullish Percent Index ($BPCOMPQ)

NYSE Bullish Percent Index ($BPNYA)

S&P 100 Bullish Percent Index ($BPOEX)

S&P 500 Bullish Percent Index ($BPSPX)

S&P Consumer Discretionary Bullish Percent Index ($BPDISC)

S&P Consumer Staples Sector Bullish Percent Index ($BPSTAP)

S&P Energy Sector Bullish Percent Index ($BPENER)

S&P Financial Sector Bullish Percent Index ($BPFINA)

S&P Healthcare Sector Bullish Percent Index ($BPHEAL)

S&P Industrials Sector Bullish Percent Index ($BPINDY)

S&P Materials Sector Bullish Percent Index ($BPMATE)

S&P Technology Sector Bullish Percent Index ($BPINFO)

S&P Telecom Services Sector Bullish Percent Index ($BPTELE)

S&P Utilities Sector Bullish Percent Index ($BPUTIL)

With that said, you need to know that The Bullish Percent chart differs from that of a PNF chart of an ETF or any other investment.

I like to describe the chart as a football field sitting in an upright position with the "goal line" at the top and the other "goal line" at the bottom.

The only thing different from a real football field is that the bottom "goal line" is the "zero-yard-line," and the top "goal line" is the "100-yard line."

The 100 (as are all the numbers on the chart) is a percentage number, so 100% of the components of the S&P 500 are in columns of Xs. If the chart is at 50, that means 50% of the components are in Xs and 50% in Os columns.

You will get the idea when we look at a Bullish Percent chart on the next page.

Bullish Percent charts rarely ever get to 100 or down to 0.

What you will find is that most columns will range between somewhere around the 70 "yard line" (percent) on the top and somewhere around the 30 "yard line" (percent) on the bottom.

On the next chart is the current Bullish Percent of the S&P 500:

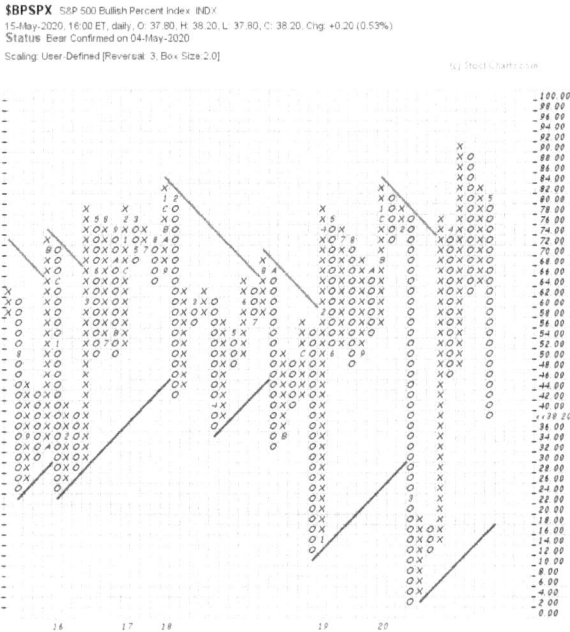

$BPSPX S&P 500 Bullish Percent Index INDX
15-May-2020, 16:00 ET, daily, O: 37.80, H: 38.20, L: 37.80, C: 38.20, Chg: +0.20 (0.53%)
Status Bear Confirmed on 04-May-2020

Scaling: User-Defined [Reversal: 3, Box Size: 2.0]

As you can see, there has been a lot of volatility in 2020.

Wide swings, from a low of 2 (%) in March to a high of 90 (%) in April; what this tells me that the S&P 500 has gone from a "buy" (below the 30-yard line) in March to a "sell" (above the 70-yard line) in April represented by the right slants at the top of the chart.

This wide swing in such a short time is unusual; however, I think we can all agree that these are not usual times!

What this chart is telling us is that 1) It is in a column of Os (sellers) and that, 2) the percentage is nearing the "30-yard" line, below which we look for the S&P 500 to go higher.

We are basically where we suspect that stocks are going higher, a general idea of where stocks are, and a logical first place to the big picture.

Investors can be well informed by looking at the Bullish Percentage chart once or twice a month.

So how did we do with our list of ingredients of the perfect investment?

1. **Liquidity?** Yes, we can get into cash in one day.
2. **Diversification?** Yes, we are in 8 of the largest markets available.
3. **Simple?** Yes, what buyers and sellers are doing.
4. **Lack of correlation?** Yes, as much as is possible.
5. **Clear buy and sell signals?** Yes.
6. **Easy to manage?** Yes, on average, less than five trades per year.

7. **Low fees?** Yes, average fees have been 1.5% to 2.5%.

8. **Performance?** Yes, over 20%/year.

Chapter 8
Performance

I just laid out before you a must-do, basic strategy for any investor.

The next obvious question is: How does this strategy perform?

Not to avoid the important question of performance, because it is a good question; there are several answers.

The first is that each investor will experience different results depending on their interpretation of the PNF charts and their decisions.

Plus, each investor's performance will vary depending on how the market(s) they invest in, and when they enter and exit those markets.

My preference is to invest in all seven of the sectors I have identified and discussed above; however, sometimes no definitive direction in a market is clear. I patiently wait until I see an agreement with the three charts we discussed earlier in those cases.

I divide the total amount I have to invest equally in each of these seven markets. For example, if I have $7,000 to invest, I allocate $1,000 in each because I don't know which one of the seven is going to be best.

That strategy takes the risk out of my portfolio because of the built-in diversification; however, it has a negative impact on my up-side potential, as some sectors may not perform and others.

The ideal scenario with this allocation is that all seven are profitable in the same year, possible, but not likely.

With that said, my overall performance since I develop the three charts to determine which ETF to use, the ETF or the Inverse ETF, has been just over 20% over each of the last five years.

However, my work supporters have pointed out that comparing my results to the S&P 500 is probably not a fair comparison since my portfolio has so much more diversification.

It remains my goal to outperform the stock market.

The portfolio of all seven sectors is probably best compared to a Balanced Mutual fund.

The long-term performance of Balanced Mutual funds ranges between 7% and 9%.

The +20% I have enjoyed is well above performing balanced funds, so I plan to stay with this strategy and always look for ways to improve performance.

There you have it; a step-by-step plan to ensure that you are on the "right" side of a market. If a market is trending up, the charts will direct you to the ETF. If the chart is in a downtrend, you will be directed to be in the Inverse ETF.

All three PNF charts need to agree, all three to ensure investment success.

Remember, treat each market separately. Each market reacts independently. Old rules of correlation don't seem to matter as much as they did 20-30 years ago.

In years past when gold would go up, for example, so did crude oil. That isn't true in today's marketplace.

The goal of my work is to increase the chances of investors being in ETF's with other buyers when buyers are dominating a market and recognizing when to invest in an Inverse ETF when sellers dominate a market.

I wish I could wave a magic wand and give you the experience I have gained from looking at literally millions of PNF charts over the past thirty years.

Since that cannot be the case, my recommendation is to begin your journey now and remember that it doesn't matter when you start or what market.

Be persistent and study PNF charts regularly. Look at as many as you can every day.

What you will discover is that there are patterns; patterns that repeat themselves. And what has been said so many times, repetition is the Mother of All Learning.

When all else fails, I am a teacher, a coach, an investment coach. I want to help you reach your goals, and to do that, we both need to continue learning. My work continues to evolve. Let's evolve and grow together.

I can always be reached at my email address:

terry@theinvestmentcompass.com

I'd love to hear from you.

About the Author

Terry J. Atzen is an author, world-traveler, financial coach, investment strategist, and founder of TIC™.

Mr. Atzen has a broad and diversified background with over fifty years in both the pharmaceutical industry and the financial services industry. His focus is on market strategies, marketing, and investment coaching. He has gained national recognition for his performance and service in each of these disciplines.

terry@theinvestmentcompass.com

Terry J. Atzen

www.ingramcontent.com/pod-product-compliance
Lightning Source LLC
Chambersburg PA
CBHW060628210326
41520CB00010B/1522